# MONEY.

BY

CHARLES MORAN.

"The two greatest inventions of the human mind are writing and money,—the common language of intelligence, and the common language of self-interest."
MARQUIS DE MIRABEAU.

NEW YORK:
D. APPLETON AND COMPANY,
443 & 445 BROADWAY.
LONDON: 16 LITTLE BRITAIN.
1863.

# PREFACE.

Notes originally commenced to be used in discussions at the meetings of the Society for the Advancement of Political and Social Science, lately organized in this city, gradually assumed the form of the present work, which is an attempt to analyze and discuss the subject of Money, in its most important, practical phases, more fully than has been done in any of the works that have, as yet, fallen into the hands of the writer.

The conclusions arrived at appear to explain and reconcile all the anomalies that, heretofore, have rendered money so vexed a subject. The views expressed in this work in regard to the relative value of gold and silver, and the effects of the large influx of gold from new mines, were published in the local press as early as 1851. Every prediction then made on this subject has been fully realized, while not one of those made by the partisans of the theory of the future depreciation of gold and appreciation of silver has been fulfilled. The conclusions in regard to the effect on prices, of bank-note issues, were arrived at and communicated to friends long before reading the able works of Fullarton and Tooke, in which similar views are maintained. This is mentioned here, not so much to claim the merit of originality for these conclusions, as with a view to obtain for them the weight due to conclusions arrived at by different parties, examining the same subject from different points of view.

The constantly increasing division of labor daily increases the exchanges of commodities and services, in which money plays so important a part. The subject of money is, therefore, supposed by the writer to be of sufficient general interest to warrant the publication of the present work. If it shall aid in dissipating any of the numerous errors and prejudices so long connected with money, and thus increase the power of this instrument to further the well-being and progress of humanity, the object of the writer will be attained and his labors amply compensated.

NEW YORK, *April* 20, 1863.

# CONTENTS.

CHAPTER I.



CHAPTER II.



CHAPTER III.



CHAPTER IV.



CHAPTER V.

CHAPTER VI.



CHAPTER VII.



CHAPTER VIII.



CHAPTER IX.



CHAPTER X.



CHAPTER XI.



CHAPTER XII.

# MONEY.

## CHAPTER I.

A CORRECT appreciation of the functions of money and of the natural laws that govern it, is of vast importance to humanity, from its universal use in the exchanges of commodities and services ; exchanges becoming each day more numerous and indispensable in consequence of the constantly increasing division of labor.

Many things have been used at different times as money : cowrie shells in Africa ; wampum by the American Indians ; cattle in ancient Greece. The Carthaginians used leather as money, probably bearing some mark or stamp. Frederic II, at the siege of Milan, issued stamped leather as money. In 1360, John the Good, King of France, who was taken prisoner by the celebrated Black Prince and sent to England until ransomed, also issued leather money, having a small silver nail in the centre. Salt is the common money in

Abyssinia; codfish in Iceland and Newfoundland. "Living money," slaves and oxen, passed current with the Anglo-Saxons, in payment of debts.* Adam Smith says that in his day there was a village in Scotland where it was not uncommon for workmen to carry nails instead of money to the baker's shop and the alehouse.† Marco Polo found, in China, money made of the bark of the mulberry tree, bearing the stamp of the sovereign, which it was death to counterfeit. Tobacco was generally used as money in Virginia up to 1660, fifty-seven years after the foundation of that colony. In 1641 the Legislature of Massachusetts enacted that wheat should be received in payment of all debts; and the Convention in France, during the Revolution, on a proposition of Jean-Bon-Saint André, long discussed the propriety of adopting wheat as money, as the measure of value of all things.‡ Platina was coined in Russia from 1828 to 1845.§ But the metals best adapted and most generally used as coin are copper, nickel, silver, and gold; the two first being now used for coins of small value, to make change, and the two latter, commonly designated "the precious metals," as measures of value and as legal tenders. On the continent of Europe, a composition of silver and copper, called billon, has long been used for small coins, which are made current at a much higher value than that of the metals they contain. In China, Sycee silver is the principal currency, and is merely ingot silver of an uniform fineness, paid and received by weight. Spanish

* Westminster Review, January 1, 1848.

† Wealth of Nations, vol. i, p. 31.

‡ Dic. d'Économie Politique, Paris, Monnaie.

§ Idem.

dollars also circulate there, but only after they have been essayed and stamped as proof that they are of the standard fineness.*

As Asia Minor produced gold, its earliest coinage was of that metal. Italy and Sicily possessing copper, bronze was first coined there. Herodotus says the Lydians were the first people known to have coined gold and silver. They had gold coins at the close of the ninth century B. C.; Greece Proper only at the close of the eighth century B. C. Servius Tullius, King of Rome, made the pound weight of copper current money. The Romans first coined silver 281 B. C., and gold 207 B. C.

At the time of the invasion of Britain by Cæsar, the ancient Britons had coins of tin, iron, brass, and gold. The Anglo-Saxons coined silver and brass, but the Norman monarchs rejected the latter, and for a long time silver was the sole metal coined. William the Conqueror issued no coins but silver pennies or "sterlings." Henry III first coined gold, in pennies weighing $\frac{1}{120}$th of a pound tower, which passed for 20*d*. Henry VII first coined silver shillings. Silver halfpence and farthings were coined from the time of Edward I to Edward VI. Their small size, particu-

* "There is no coined silver or gold currency in China; the only money taken being a copper coin, called cash, of small value, 1,700 representing a Spanish Carolus dollar. Silver, therefore, in bulk, at its pure touch of 100 per cent., takes the place of a coined measure of value, being divided into the Government standard weights called tael, mace, cash, candareem, each having a decimal proportion to the other; and thus a nominal money is created, although more properly these terms are merely 'denominations of weight.'" (Report of Mr. Consul Robertson on the trade of the port of Shanghai for the year 1855, quoted in Tooke's History of Prices, vol. vi, p. 679.)

larly after the reduction of the weight of the silver coins, caused them to be discontinued; and James I directed farthing tokens of brass and copper to be struck, but they were of such inferior value that they soon fell into disuse. The first copper coinage in England was in 1672, under Charles II, who also coined tin in 1684. James II attempted to give currency to gun metal and pewter, but the attempt was soon given up. Henry VII, in 1489, coined the first sovereigns, of gold 23 carats 3½ fine. Henry VIII, in 1544, coined half, quarter, and eighth sovereigns, of the present standard of 22 carats fine. Charles II, in 1675, coined the first guinea, called thus because made of African gold.

In 1797, during the suspension of the Bank of England, the deficiency of the silver coinage was so great in England, that it was attempted to be supplied by the issue of Spanish dollars, stamped with the mark of the king's head. They were issued at 4*s.* 9*d.*, but were called in again in the course of the year; but the practice was resumed at various periods during the war. In 1811 the Bank of England was permitted to strike and issue silver tokens, to pass current for 5*s.* 6*d.*, 3*s.*, and 1*s.* 6*d.*[*]

The sovereigns of Europe extensively falsified the moneys they coined, by diminishing their weight and the fineness of the metal they were made of, to facilitate the liquidation of their debts. Under Servius Tullius, 550 B. C., the as or pondo contained a Roman pound of copper. In 175 B. C. it had been reduced to ½ oz. or $\frac{1}{24}$th part of its original weight. The livre in France,

* Macleod, Theory and Practice of Banking, vol. i, p. 168.

under Charlemagne, contained 12 ounces of pure silver, but was gradually reduced by his successors, particularly by Philip le Bel * and by the first sovereigns of the house of Valois. John the Good made seventy-one alterations in the value of the coin in nine years, alternately increasing and decreasing the quantity of pure metal it contained. For example, by an edict of November 27, 1359, the marc of pure silver was ordered to be coined into 18 livres ; by an edict of January 22, 1360, into 54 livres ; March 21, 1360, into 125 livres ; March 31, 1360, into 12 livres ; April 25, 1360, into 16 livres ; May 28, 1360, into 12 livres ; June 29, 1360, into 20 livres ; &c., &c.† To appreciate fully the effects of these fluctuations in the value of the coin, it must be remembered that after a currency has been for a time depreciated, as much injustice is done by raising, as was previously done by depressing its value. Philip le Bel

* "In January, 1311, a new debasement of the coin, which lasted until September, 1313, reduced the livre to frs. 13.66. This standard was followed by another that raised the livre to frs. 18.37, which was established at the moment when an extraordinary subsidy was to be levied, to which Philip le Bel became entitled by the custom of those times, on the occasion of his eldest son's being made a knight. Philip le Bel, at his death, left the livre at about $\frac{10}{11}$ths of its value at the moment of his accession to the throne, but in the mean time he had caused it to alter in value twenty-two times in the last nineteen years of his reign! He had designed to reëstablish the finances, whereas he only succeeded in destroying many private fortunes, in causing the royal authority to fall into contempt, in exciting intestine hatreds, and in producing a bloody riot in the streets of Paris." (Natalis Wailly, Researches on the Monetary System of St. Louis, quoted in the Journal des Economistes of Paris, September, 1862.)

Dante says of Philip le Bel:

"La si vedra il duol che sopra Senna
Induce, falseggiando la moneta." (Par. xix.)

† E. Cartier, Revue Numismatique of Paris, 1838, pp. 104–108.

coined gold 22 carats fine; Philip de Valois coined it 23, 22, and 21 carats fine; John the Good, 21 and 18 carats fine. Charles V, surnamed the Wise, restored the coin to a fixed weight and fineness, under the advice of Nicole Oresme, Bishop of Lisieux, who wrote an admirable treatise, published both in Latin and French, on the origin, nature, functions, and mutations of money, in which he says: "If the truth were not maintained in regard to the weight and fineness of the coin, it would be a vile falsehood and a fradulent deception. It is just and proper for a sovereign to condemn and punish false coiners. But what if he himself commits that which it is his duty to punish with death in others? The coin does not belong to the sovereign, but to those who possess it. Neither sovereign nor state has the right to alter the value, weight, or fineness of money. The effigy of the sovereign or the stamp on the coin is a proof of its weight and quality. A sovereign who alters the value of the coin in weight or fineness is a liar, commits perjury, and bears false testimony." * The falsification of the coin was, however, continued in France till the beginning of the reign of Louis XV. The reduction of the livre from 1497 to 1602 was from 2,225 to 1,208 centigrammes of pure silver. In 1789 the livre only contained $\frac{100}{7885}$ths of the pure silver it contained in the time of Charlemagne.

In England the coin was also debased by the sovereigns. From the Conquest to the present time, however, all the English silver coins are of the standard of 11 oz. 2 dwts. fine and 18 dwts. alloy, except for the short period of sixteen years, from the 34th Henry VIII

* Journal des Economistes, Paris, September, 1862, pp. 372, 373.

to the 2d Elizabeth, during which the standard was greatly debased. "Henry VIII stands recorded with infamy as the first English sovereign who debased the sterling fineness of the coins."* The shilling of William the Conqueror contained $266\frac{4}{10}$ grains tower or $249\frac{3}{4}$ grains troy of pure silver. It was reduced by Edward VI, in 1550, to $21\frac{1}{3}$ grains tower or 20 grains troy. In 1552 it was made to contain $94\frac{3}{10}$ grains tower or $88\frac{4}{10}$ grains troy. The English mint used the tower pound until the 18th Henry VIII, when it was replaced by the troy pound, which has been used ever since, and is $\frac{3}{4}$ oz. heavier than the tower pound.

The following table exhibits the various modifications made in the silver coinage of England :

| | Standard, or fine silver, in pound of 12 oz. | Standard silver coined into per pound Tower. | Standard silver coined into per pound Troy. | Grains Troy of standard silver in one penny. | Grains Troy of fine silver in one penny. |
|---|---|---|---|---|---|
| Conquest, A. D. 1066 | 11 oz. 2 dwt. | 20s. 0d. | | 22½ | 20.81 |
| 28 Edward I, " 1300 | " | 20 3 | | 22¼ | 20.55 |
| 18 Edward III, " 1344 | " | 22 2 | | 20¼ | 18.68 |
| 20 " " 1346 | " | 22 6 | | 20 | 18.50 |
| 25 " " 1350 | " | 25 6 | | 18 | 16.65 |
| 13 Henry IV, " 1412 | " | 30 0 | | 15 | 13.87 |
| 4 Edward IV, " 1464 | " | 37 6 | | 12 | 11.10 |
| 18 Henry VIII, " 1526 | " | 42 2¼=45s. 0d. | | 10⅝ | 9.87 |
| 34 " " 1543 | 10 oz. 0 dwt. | | 48 0 | 10 | 8.33 |
| 36 " " 1544 | 6 0 | | 48 0 | 10 | 5 — |
| 37 " " 1545 | 4 0 | | 48 0 | 10 | 3.33 |
| 3 Edward VI, " 1549 | 6 0 | | 72 0 | 6⅝ | 3.33 |
| 4 " " 1550 | 3 0 | | 72 0 | 6⅝ | 1.67 |
| 6 " " 1552 | 11 1 | | 60 0 | 8 | 7.37 |
| 1 Elizabeth, " 1558 | 11 2 | | 60 0 | 8 | 7.50 |
| 43 " " 1601 | 11 2 | | 62 0 | 7¾ | 7.16 |
| 56 George III, " 1816 | 11 2 | | 64 0 | 7¼ | 6.727 |

Pure gold is said to be 24 carats fine. The carat is an Abyssinian weight divided into 4 grains, and the grains into quarters. A carat grain is equivalent to

* Ruding, Annals of Coinage, vol. i, p. 300.

$2\frac{1}{2}$ dwts. When gold coins were first made at the English mint, the standard of the gold put in them was $23\frac{1}{2}$ carats $3\frac{1}{2}$ grains fine, and $\frac{1}{2}$ grain alloy ; and so it continued without any variation to the 18th Henry VIII, who in that year first introduced a new standard of 22 carats fine and 2 carats alloy. Henry VIII made his gold coins of both these standards, and this practice was continued by his successors until 1633. From that period to the present time, the gold of which the coins of England have been made has invariably been of the new standard of 22 carats fine. Standard gold has been coined in England since 1717 into 3*l.* 17*s.* $10\frac{1}{2}$*d.* per oz. By the act of 1844, the Bank of England is obligated to purchase all the gold bullion and foreign coins of standard fineness at 3*l.* 17*s.* 9*d.* per oz.

The debasement of the coins was universal during the middle ages. In Scotland, previous to 1296, the pound of silver was coined into 20 shillings. In 1601, £36 or 720 shillings, were coined out of the same quantity. The gold ducat or sequin, when first coined in Venice in 1284, was equivalent to 3 Italian livres ; to-day it would be worth 22 livres. The florin, originally a gold coin of the value of about 10 shillngs sterling ($2.50), is now a silver coin worth about 20 pence sterling (40 cents). The Spanish coin maravedi, in 1220 weighed 24 grammes (370 grains troy) of gold ; it is now a small copper coin equal to $\frac{43}{272}$ of an English penny. The Russian rouble of 1700 is worth $2\frac{70}{100}$ of the roubles of 1821.

## CHAPTER II.

It was the constant alteration by the sovereigns of the weight and fineness of the coins, as well as their depreciation by wear and by clipping, that gave rise to the ideal money of account of the banks of Venice, Genoa, Amsterdam, Hamburg, &c. These institutions received all kinds of coin on deposit, but only credited the depositors with their actual weight of fine metal, by reducing them to the weight and fineness of their ideal money of account. These moneys of account were alone received in payment of debts due to the banks, and, for a long time, were at a considerable premium. The reason for this premium is very evident from the fact that the general average value of the coins circulating in Amsterdam in 1609, when the Bank of Amsterdam was founded, was 9 per cent. below their standard value.* The certificates of deposit issued by these banks, finally suggested the use of bank bills as money. The first bank bills that circulated as money were those of the Bank of Stockholm, established in 1668. They were mere receipts for coin deposited with the bank, but by a law of 1726, they were made receivable in payment of all bills of exchange.

* Encyc. Britannica, Money.

The first institution, however, that was legally authorized to issue bank bills payable to bearer at sight, was the Bank of England, founded in 1694.

There is to-day a greater difference of opinion on the subject of money, than on almost any other subject treated of by the economists. Bastiat, in his little pamphlet entitled "Maudit Argent," makes an economist say: "I curse money because it is constantly confounded with wealth, and from this confusion arise errors and calamities without number. I curse it because its functions are ill understood and very difficult of comprehension. I curse it because it confuses all ideas, causes the means to be mistaken for the end, the obstacle for the cause, alpha for omega; because its presence in the world, beneficial in itself, has introduced a false notion, a begging of the question, a fallacious theory that, in its numerous ramifications, has impoverished man, and encrimsoned the earth with blood. I curse it because I feel myself incapable of wrestling against the errors to which it has given birth, otherwise than by a long and fastidious dissertation to which no one will listen."

To appreciate clearly the functions of money and the natural laws that govern it, it becomes necessary to establish a few preliminary principles.

Wealth and utility are synonymous terms—so are value and capital. But wealth and capital—utility and value—are not synonymous terms, although constantly used as such by most persons. It is not the utility of a thing itself that constitutes its value, but the *usefulness* (not the *amount*) of the human labor and intelligence incorporated in the thing at the time when it is sold. Water is indispensable to man, and yet water has actually no value, notwithstanding its great utility. But the labor of bringing water from a distance to the hands of those who need it, has to be remunerated, and this often gives value to water. In such a case, the price paid for the water is the mere remuneration of the human labor incorporated in the water, and thus saved to the purchaser. The water itself is one of the innumerable bounties bestowed on man by the Creator, all of which ever remain gratuitous, no matter through how many hands they may pass, except when human monopolies, the fruit of human laws, intervene.

The labor incorporated on things, and thus saved to those who acquire them, is what constitutes value or capital. Nothing is capital but the existing results of previous labor that can contribute to man's enjoyment and well being. This analysis of capital shows the correctness of the theory of Bastiat, that all exchanges are mere exchanges of services.

Money is not capital, but a mere representative of capital, although the material of which it is made may be capital when not used as money. Capital is sought with a view to be consumed or retained, whereas money is only sought as means of obtaining useful commodities and services ; in other words, men seek money only because it is universally accepted in exchange for commodities and services, which it therefore represents. But representatives are constantly confounded with the things they represent, and this is particularly the case with gold and silver and paper money. In consequence of having been at first used as commodities, at their value for consumption, although now generally used as representatives of capital, as means of obtaining commodities and services, the precious metals are still generally looked upon as capital itself—in fact, as the only true capital.* This is carried to such an extent that we are elated at an arrival of $1,000,000 in coin from any quarter; while we are alarmed at an arrival of $5,000,000 in commodities indispensable to the welfare of the community, because we fear it may lead to the exportation of a portion of our dearly prized gold and silver, in exchange for the commodities; and yet it is evident that the only use of coin or money is to obtain with it the things useful to humanity! Of what use is money where there are no commodities or services to exchange? The idea that money alone is real capital or wealth, has undoubtedly diminished the general welfare and progress of humanity, by diverting its attention from industry, the sole source of all capital. The same idea originated the celebrated mercantile system,† first introduced by the Emperor

* "Gold and silver being useful for other purposes besides serving for currency, have a certain intrinsic value, and for that reason alone they are, to a certain extent, wealth in themselves. Many persons who cannot discriminate the simple ideas involved in one complex one, entertain very erroneous opinions on this subject, and are apt to consider *money* and *wealth* as convertible terms. *Gold and silver, however, derive their chief value from their peculiar fitness to form a currency*, and they are less useful for general purposes than almost any other metal." (Macleod, Theory and Practice of Banking, vol. i, p. 35.)

† "According to the crude ideas that were generally received about a century ago, gold and silver were almost universally considered to be nearly the only species of wealth, and it was considered to be the true policy of every country to encourage, by every means in its power, the influx of bullion, and to discourage its export; and most, if not all, of the European nations have gone so far, at one time or another, as to prohibit its export.

Charles V, in the relations between Spain and her colonies, and subsequently introduced by Colbert in the relations between nations ; a system most injurious to all, and yet gradually adopted by all nations, and still retained by them to a greater or lesser extent.

It is evidently this idea, that gold and silver are the only true wealth, that induced England, since the 18th Charles II, to coin the precious metals without charge to the owners of the bullion deposited at the mint—a custom which has most improperly become general among nations ; for coining money is a service rendered to the owners of bullion, who should, therefore, bear the expense, and not the community at large. Mr. Mushet, in his evidence before a committee of the House of Lords in 1819, stated that gold could be coined at the English mint for one half of one per cent., and silver probably for one and a half per cent. In France the expense of coining has been reduced for gold to 6 francs for every 3,100 francs, or 0.193 per cent.; for silver, to 75 centimes for every 100 francs, or $\frac{3}{4}$ per cent. In Russia it costs $\frac{35}{100}$ per cent. for gold and

The profit of foreign commerce was estimated solely by the quantity of gold and silver it brought into the country; and the theory of commerce seemed to be reduced to a general scramble among all nations, to see which could draw to itself most gold and silver from the others. According to this theory, the gain of one party was the loss of the other; every article produced in another country, and imported into this one, was considered a direct loss to the country. This was what was called the mercantile or commercial system."

"So far from the principle of the mercantile theory being true, that gold and silver are the most profitable and desirable object of import, the direct reverse is unquestionably true, that gold and silver are, of all objects of commerce, the most unprofitable." (Macleod, Theory and Practice of Banking, vol. i, pp. 297–299.)

$2\frac{95}{100}$ per cent. for silver.* In the United States † the estimated expense of coinage is :

| | | | |
|---|---|---|---|
| At Philadelphia, $2\frac{23}{100}$ | per cent., all metals included. | | |
| New Orleans, $6\frac{68}{100}$ | " | " | " |
| North Carolina, 9 | " | " | " |
| Georgia, $9\frac{97}{100}$ | " | " | " |

Man, in his operations for his own individual account, rarely commits the error of confounding capital and its representatives, because this would be fatal to his own well being. An individual never borrows money to retain it as direct means of enjoyment : he invariably seeks money as means of obtaining, by exchange, those things which contribute, *per se*, to his enjoyment or well being. An intelligent man never long retains money on hand. He invariably exchanges it for useful or productive things. But in their collective capacity, as legislators and theorists, where the results of their actions and theories fall principally upon others, men constantly assert and act on the theory that capital and money are identical.‡

Of all the representatives of capital and services, gold and silver have been the most generally used. They were undoubtedly first resorted to by merchants as mediums of exchanging commodities, from their general use for ornaments, which gave them a current value everywhere. The scarcity of these metals also gave

* Encyc. Britannica, Money.

† Report of Committee on Commerce of House of Representatives, September, 1850.

‡ " Gold and silver, though they serve for few, yet they command all the conveniencies of life, and *therefore in a plenty of them consists riches.*" (Locke, vol. v, p. 12, London edition, 1823.)

them a great value in a small volume, another great advantage they offered as means of exchanging commodities. At first the value of gold and silver was entirely regulated by their value at the silversmith's, for merchants then only used the precious metals as commodities, easily bartered everywhere for any other commodity desired ; and as long as this was the case, their value followed the same law as the value of other commodities. But experience having demonstrated that gold and silver were admirable instruments for facilitating the exchanges of commodities and services, they were each day more and more used for that purpose alone, without the slightest view to consumption ; and this change in their use, from commodities for consumption to mere counters representing commodities delivered or services rendered, was so gradual and imperceptible that to this day it is generally believed, even by economists of eminence, that the value of gold and silver entirely depends on their intrinsic value, or on the amount of labor required to produce them.* But this evidently is an error, for as soon as the use of gold and silver as coin, as representatives of commodities, became infinitely greater than their use as commodities, their value as coin, as instruments of exchanges, regulated

* Mr. Senior, in one of his lectures on the value of money, observes: "The value of the precious metals, as money, must depend ultimately on their value as materials of jewelry and plate ; since if they were not used as commodities, they could not circulate as money." (Tooke, History of Prices, vol. v, p. 224.)

Mr. Senior had evidently in view only the original cause which led to the use of the precious metals—of their use as commodities easily bartered everywhere : he entirely ignored their use as counters representing commodities and services.

their value as commodities. Should either metal ever be more useful or more sought for as a commodity than as money, it would soon disappear from circulation as coin, no matter what efforts might be made to retain it as coin; but so long as they are mostly used as money, gold and silver as commodities will always be worth the value given them as coin, the delay and expense of coining alone deducted; for no one will ever sell the precious metals as bullion, at less than their value as coin, so long as they can be coined and used as money; nor will any cne ever pay more for gold and silver as commodities, than their value as coin, so long as they can be obtained by melting the coin. This is well established by the fact that all the precious metals used in the arts are paid the exact value, neither more nor less, that they are worth as money.

*As commodities, gold and silver are capital; but as money, they are mere representatives of commodities, of capital itself.* It is this double function of gold and silver, as commodities and as representatives of commodities, that has confused all the economists and writers on the subject of the precious metals. And it is from not separating, from confounding these two opposite and entirely different attributes of the precious metals, that have arisen most of the erroneous theories in regard to their value.* It is from considering metallic money as capital that Macleod arrives at the absurd conclusion that credit is capital.† "Money is capital—money

* "But there will be found to be no inconsiderable difference, if we distinguish as we ought to do, for the purpose whether of theory or practice, between gold considered as merchandise, i. e., capital, and gold considered as currency, circulating in the shape of coin among the public." (Tooke, History of Prices, vol. iii, p. 224.)

† Theory and Practice of Banking, vol. i, p. 262: "Hence as capital and

commands and exchanges commodities and services—so does credit to a still greater extent—therefore credit as well as money is capital." That this is the process of reasoning by which he arrives at this absurd conclusion, is very evident from the fact that he says,* "a credit perform exactly the same functions and are essentially of the same nature—*the one being the symbol of past labor, the other of future labor,* but both being transferring power, it is not an incorrect expression to say that CREDIT IS CAPITAL."

* Theory and Practice of Banking, vol. i, p. 259. Macleod's extraordinary theory that credit is capital, comes also from his employing the term capital in its mercantile sense, as designating money, instead of in its scientific sense, as designating all economized, existing results of labor. He says, vol. i, p. 262: "What is capital in the ordinary sense? It is that portion of currency which is employed in reproductive operations: when the harvest is reaped, part of the corn is consumed and part is sown again. Now currency is like corn, the part that is consumed is revenue, and the part that is sown again is capital." Here are two important errors: 1. Capital held idle is just as much capital as when used in reproductive operations. The idea that nothing is capital that is not used reproductively, is one of the exploded errors of the earlier economists, an error arising from the mercantile sense of the term capital. 2. What part of currency is consumed? and by what process? Until Mr. Macleod answers these queries we cannot admit that currency is consumed like corn, either productively or unproductively.

Macleod seems to look upon labor as productive only of money wages, for he says, vol. ii, p. xliv: "But suppose that instead of spending all his earnings on commodities, he saves a portion, . . . that saving is called capital." The only capital produced by the laborer, that can become an addition to previously existing capital, is the result of his labor—money, whether metallic or paper, is only an instrument which, like the highway or the wagon, aids the transfer of commodities from one person or place to another; and the money, exactly like the highway or the wagon, must be in existence before it can be used to facilitate exchanges. Consequently, in no way can any portion of money wages saved by a laborer be an addition to existing capital. How Macleod should have fallen into the error of using the term *capital* as synonymous with money is really incomprehensible, for he says, vol. ii, p. xlv, "The primary, genuine, and exclusive meaning of capital is the accumulated savings of labor, and its *symbol* is money."

banker's notes in circulation are quite as much banking capital to him as gold deposited with him by his creditors." How can a banker's indebtedness be capital to him ?

The metal contained in a coin is a commodity before it is coined, and also after it is melted ; but as long as it is used as money, to facilitate the exchanges of commodities and services, it is a mere counter, a representative of commodities and services, no more subject to the laws that govern commodities and services than paper money.* For example, increase the representatives of commodities and services, and in no way will it increase the enjoyment and progress of the community. On the contrary, increase the amount of commodities and services available to the community, and the well being of all will be increased, no matter how little money there may be ; for the absence of money would only render the exchanges of commodities less rapid and easy, but it would not prevent the general enjoyment and progress produced by commodities and services. Civilization is possible without money, but civilization is perfectly impossible without the commodities and services that contribute to man's progress and well being. This seems to have been clearly perceived by the

How can a symbol be *bona fide* capital ? Capital always designates something real, something useful, *per se*. Macleod says himself, vol. ii, p. liv: "It is true that capital is not exactly synonymous with money ; but money is its symbol and representative."

* "Money of every kind is an order for goods ; it is so considered by the laborer when he receives it, and is almost instantly turned into money's worth. It is merely the instrument by which the purchasable stock of the country is distributed with convenience and advantage among the several members of the community." (Thornton, An Inquiry, &c., p. 260, quoted by Macleod, Theory and Practice of Banking, vol. i, p. 390.)

celebrated Marshal Vauban, who said, "the true wealth of a kingdom consists in the abundance of products useful to man." Also by Voltaire, who said: "A nation that should have only gold and silver, would be most miserable, whilst a nation that possessed none of these metals, but produced all other things that contribute to man's enjoyment and welfare, would be very wealthy."

Money is the measure of value of all things *except itself.* But in this world there is nothing absolute; all is relative. Therefore money does not, cannot measure the absolute or intrinsic value of things, but merely their relative value; or rather, the momentary estimation of the relative usefulness of the human labor and intelligence incorporated in things. And money measures this relation, not because it contains in itself an equivalent amount of usefulness or labor, but because it is everywhere accepted at a fixed value in exchange for all other things. When $2 are paid for a pair of shoes, and $4 for a hat, it does not indicate that the hat and the shoes contain the same amount of human labor as the silver or the gold contained in the coins, or the paper on which are printed the bank notes, given for them. It indicates, merely, that it requires two pairs of shoes to purchase one hat—in other words, that the human labor incorporated in one hat is as much prized as that incorporated in two pairs of shoes —that with one hat the hatter can purchase two pairs of shoes, and "*vice versa.*"

Anything that is not generally accepted in exchange for commodities and services, cannot perform the functions of money, no matter how great be the amount of human labor required to produce or procure the material it is made of. A counterfeit coin, almost worthless, and even a counterfeit bank note, entirely worthless, successfully perform all the functions of money as long as they are accepted in exchange for commodities and services.*

All commercial nations now use either one or both of the precious metals as money. They are supposed to give them a fixed value by coining them and making them a legal tender in payment of all taxes levied by the Government that coins them, and of all individual

* "Coin is an ordinary commodity, like any other, authenticated as to quality and weight by the stamp of the state. But coin, so long as it circulates within the realm for the purpose of buying and selling, *loses for the time its intrinsic value.* It resembles a steam engine, a field, or any other machine. Its intrinsic value is suspended till it is sold, and *its worth consists solely in the work it achieves.* Sovereigns, when passing from hand to hand, are no better than counters or tokens. They are not wanted for the sake of the gold they contain, but simply as pledges that a man shall be able to buy with them as many commodities as those he gave in exchange for them. A bad shilling does the work of coin quite as well as a good one till it is found out; and it then becomes worthless, because the absence of the intrinsic value destroys faith in its power to persuade a seller to part with his wares. If that seller knew that he could pass it off as good upon another man, he would (apart from the question of morality) be as willing to take it as a silver shilling. *Metallic money, whilst acting as coin, is identical with paper money, in respect of being destitute of intrinsic value;* with this single difference, that when it is desired to reproduce that intrinsic value, the sovereign can be instantly turned into bullion; whilst, in the case of a note, an intermediate step is necessary—it must be sent to the bank before its intrinsic worth is recovered. The security for the value is already in the hands of the holder of the sovereign; for the note, the solvency of the issuer is an additional requisite. *Still, whilst circulating, both make no use of intrinsic value; and this is the great point to grasp firmly.*" (What is Money?—*North British Review, Nov.* 1861—without exception the best article on money we have yet met with.)

contracts. But this fixed value is only illusory. *Coining money does not establish its value. It only indicates the quantity and quality of the metal of which the coins are made.** Coins are mere pieces of metal, of fixed weight and quality, tested by an authority recognised by all, with which purchases may be made and all contracts for the payment of money fulfilled. A contract to pay one thousand dollars, pounds, florins, francs, or any other coin, is simply a contract to deliver a certain number of pieces of metal of a certain weight and fineness; and the coins are such pieces, certified correct by

* "The province or function of the Government in regard to coinage, as conducted by the Mint in obedience to the prescribed regulations, is simply to certify by a stamp, bearing the effigy of the sovereign, the weight and fineness of the piece of metal to which it is applied." (Tooke, vol. v, p. 517.)

"When nations advanced beyond the stage of direct barter, and began to use the precious metals as a common measure to which the value of all other commodities was referred, it was the *weight* of the pure metal which was invariably used as the index of value, and merchants carried scales about with them, for the purpose of weighing out the metal on each separate occasion. . . . The necessity of carrying about scales to weigh out the metal on each separate occasion being felt to be tedious and irksome, the plan was devised of cutting the bullion into pieces of a certain definite weight by the public authority, and putting a stamp upon them to certify to the community that they were warranted to contain a certain weight of bullion of a certain definite fineness. Values were then estimated by the number of these pieces of bullion, which were called coins, which were given for commodities, and then they were said to be reckoned by *tale*. It is clear that the sole object of coining was to save the trouble of weighing, and that though the prices of articles were estimated in figures, it was essentially part of the understanding that these figures denote certain specific quantities of pure metal." (Macleod, Theory and Practice of Banking, vol. i, pp. 275, 276.)

"The stamp on the coin is the guarantee of the state that it contains a certain weight of bullion." (Macleod, Theory and Practice of Banking, vol. i, p. 289.)

competent authority. How unjust, then, how great the abuse of power, for a Government to debase the coin, or to make paper a legal tender, and thus force creditors to accept, in liquidation of existing contracts, something else than what the contracts stipulate! After one of the parties to a contract has fulfilled his part of it, what principle of law or equity authorizes the enactment of a law absolving the other party, in whole or in part, from fulfilling his portion of the contract? Is it not a well-established principle of legislation that no law shall be retroactive in its effect, or shall impair the obligation of existing contracts?* That coining the

* "Money has two functions: the one, that of serving as an instrument of exchange; the other, that of being the subject of contracts for future payment. It is in the latter capacity that the fixity of a standard is most essential. It is as the subject of engagements or obligations for future payment, that in every view of justice and polity, the specific thing promised, in quantity and quality, should be paid at the expiration of the term." (Tooke, History of Prices, vol. i. pp. 145, 146.)

"An alteration of the standard is a direct fraud upon debtors or creditors, according as it is raised or lowered; because the essence of every contract is, that the debtor is to pay a certain weight of gold, and not so many abstract ideas which are called pounds." (Macleod, Theory and Practice of Banking, vol. i. p. 289.)

"When one man lends another a sum of money to be returned to him at some future period, . . . he grants the use of a certain number of pieces of metal of given weight and fineness during a definite period, on condition that an equal number of pieces of the same weight and fineness shall be restored at the expiration of the time. . . . There is here no question of *value*, or what quantity of commodity or set of commodities the gold will command in exchange. This has no part in the contract. The agreement respects the *quantity* and not the *value* of the gold; it has nothing to do with the purchasing power of gold in the market. . . . This is a correct representation of the nature of all mere pecuniary bargains. . . . We must come to a *quantity* of something at last."

"It is true that contracts may be made which shall have reference to the value of gold or silver as well as to its quantity. . . . I may with great

precious metals does not give them a fixed value is very evident from the well-known fact that any given amount of money will, at one time, purchase a much greater amount of commodities than at another, although the money contains, at both moments, the same amount of metal of the same fineness. And yet it is the almost universal opinion that the only thing that retains a fixed, unalterable value is metallic currency; and this opinion, however erroneous it may be, greatly aids in giving gold and silver their universal circulation.

Money can neither be a proper measure of value, nor the proper subject of contracts for future payments, if it be subject to alterations. The only attribute of money that cannot be fixed is its exchangeable value, which can only be expressed or measured by the quantity of other things obtained in exchange for a given amount of money. Therefore, while gold and silver measure the value of commodities and services, commodities and services alone can measure the value of gold and silver.*

The use of the precious metals as money, everywhere, enables commerce to resort to them as an uni-

propriety stipulate, that, inasmuch as the £100 which I lend when wheat is at 50s. per quarter is equal to 40 quarters of wheat, the value of 40 quarters of wheat shall be returned to me when the loan is repaid. In effect this is lending the wheat. In the same way any other commodity may be lent, or any other stipulation may be made. The freedom of bargain is and ought to be quite unrestricted." (Bailey, Money and its Vicissitudes in Value—quoted by Tooke, History of Prices, vol. v. pp. 148–149.)

* "Gold and silver do not measure the value of commodities more than the latter measure the value of gold and silver. When one commodity is exchanged for another, each measures the value of the other." (Encyclopædia Britannica, Money.)

versal measure of *relative values*. By knowing the relative quantity and fineness of the metal contained in the coins of any two countries, and the money price of things in both, the relative value of anything in both countries can at once be accurately ascertained and compared. Without this knowledge a large portion of the beneficial operations of commerce and industry would be impossible.

Metallic money is supposed to carry its value in itself. This was the case at first, when it was used exclusively as a commodity. This value in itself was an indispensable attribute of money in the early stages of civilization, when it was used as a medium of exchanges between strangers, and between parties having no confidence in each other, or in the laws that protected them, and who, therefore, would not part with their property unless they received in exchange, on the spot, something of equal intrinsic value in their eyes. But to-day the most important use of money is as an acknowledgment, as a certificate, of services rendered but not yet remunerated, which the community is bound to liquidate by rendering equivalent services to the holders, on demand. Gold and silver coin must be redeemed by commodities or services on demand, or they can no more perform the functions of money than irredeemable paper money.

## CHAPTER III.

THE ancients had quite as correct ideas of money as most of the writers and theorists on the subject at the present day. Aristotle said : " May not money be an imaginary wealth ? . . . What value has it from nature ? Should public confidence or opinion, that gives it circulation, experience a change, what would be its real price ? What real want of humanity would it then supply ? Alongside of a heap of gold one might be in want of even food. What folly to call wealth a thing in the midst of which one might die of want !" Elsewhere he says, "It was agreed to give and to receive, in exchange for all things and services, a product or thing *useful in itself*, and easily handled in the ordinary transactions of life, such as iron, silver, or any other substance, of which the dimensions and weight were first determined; and finally, to avoid the trouble of continual measurages, it was stamped with a particular mark, *a sign of its value.*" The last idea is erroneous, as coining indicates quantity and quality, not value. And yet Michel Chevalier quotes this last extract as " the very correct opinion of Aristotle, *in which there is not a single word* to alter to-day ;" and he adds, "Money is a thing useful in itself, and not a sign."*

The celebrated Law seems to have had some very correct views in regard to money. He said, "Money (coin) does not receive its value from Government. The stamp it bears indicates its weight and its fineness but does not give it its value."

Le Hardy de Beaulieu, an eminent Belgian economist of the present day, says: "The value of money follows the variations of value of the metal of which it is made, and no law or change in the names of the coins can make them escape these variations." Instead of its being the value of the metal that controls the value of money, it is the value of money that governs the value of the metal of which it is made. The same author himself says: "The second cause of the value of money is entirely independent of the substance of which it is made; it results entirely from the services rendered by money in facilitating exchanges. *This value has no tendency to equalize itself to the cost of the material of which the money is made.* It depends solely on the relation between supply and demand. If a government only coined and emitted one half of the coin necessary to make the exchanges of a community, and could interdict all importations of foreign coin and the use of all representatives, the value of money could double, whatever be the intrinsic value of the material of which it is made; and *vice versa.*" But he adds, "any excess beyond the wants of the community *is invariably idle or is exported.* On the contrary if the supply be inadequate, paper representatives are resorted

* Dictionnaire de l'Economie Politique, vol. ii, p. 202.

to, so that the value of money is always kept uniform." And yet, subsequently, he says: "The excess of the supply beyond the demand is a cause of depreciation exactly like with any merchandise or product."* How can this be, if, as he says, the excess beyond the wants of the community is invariably idle or exported?

The value of all things which the wants or desires of humanity require to be produced, depends on the cost of production, and on supply and demand. A thing must be worth the cost of production, including a moderate profit to the producer, otherwise its production will cease. Cost of production is therefore the normal point around which the price of all things needed must oscillate.† Supply and demand regulate, *not*

* Traité élémentaire d'Economie Politique, pp. 133, 134.

† Macleod, in his Theory and Practice of Banking, asserts that supply and demand alone control price, and criticises in unmeasured language, all who have maintained that cost of production regulates value.‡ This is one of the remarkable errors of that very talented economist. He has probably fallen into this error from the fact that supply and demand *alone* control the price of *all things that cannot be produced at will by human efforts*, such as diamonds and precious stones, paintings of old masters, antiques, &c., &c. But these articles are entirely exceptional, and of but little importance. Prices are of importance as stimulus to effort, to the production of those things necessary and useful to humanity. The price of all things that are produced by human effort, in which human labor is incorporated, is mainly governed by the cost of production, for the moment the producer cannot obtain cost of production and a moderate profit, he ceases to produce. Macleod asserts *that value does not spring from the labor of the producer, but from the desire of the consumer.* What then remunerates and regulates labor if not the value of its results? Looking at the cost of production as the normal point, we can

‡ "The rule that cost of production regulates value, is one of the most pestilent heresies that deform and confuse the current political economy of the day. . . . We have no hesitation in saying that the whole system of political economy as laid down by Ricardo, and developed by Mr. J. S. Mill, is utterly and radically bad." (Macleod, Theory and Practice of Banking, Introduction, vol. ii, p. 63, 64.)

*the price of things*, as is generally said by the economists, but *the division of labor*, by means of the variations in the item of price called profit and loss. When left entirely free, labor and capital, under the beneficial stimulus of self-interest, have a constant tendency to transfer themselves from the least profitable, to the most remunerative, occupations. And as the production of those things most desired by the community is always the most profitable occupation, and *vice versa*, individual interests are thus constantly kept in perfect accordance with the general interest ; all things wanted are produced, and no article is long produced in excess of the wants of the consumers.

Every want of man has a limit, but the aggregate of his wants and desires is constantly increasing, and is, apparently, unlimited ; for as soon as one want or desire is satisfied, another arises. Gold and silver, therefore, *as long as used as money, as representatives of all the wants of humanity*, will remain in unlimited demand ; could they be affected by supply and demand, the greater the reduction of their exchangeable value, the greater would be the demand for them, because

foresee the future course of production, and thus regulate that important element of human well-being. If the price of any article leaves a large profit on the cost of production, its production will increase—if it leaves a loss, its production will decrease. Here is a guide for both producers and consumers, which means all humanity. Can Mr. Macleod's "fundamental truth," that "speculation is the mother of production, but demand is the origin of value,"* supply any such guide? Why is it that an article in great demand and quite scarce is worth only $1, whilst another article, not nearly as scarce, nor in as great demand, cannot be obtained under $10 or $20? It must be that the amount of labor required to produce each article has something to do with regulating its price, no matter how great the demand, or how limited the supply, of either.

* Vol. ii, p. lxiii.

every reduction of their exchangeable value, would render necessary the use of a greater amount of them to obtain any given amount of services or commodities.

Most of the economists assert that the value of the precious metals, like that of all other commodities, depends on the cost of production and supply and demand.* On the contrary, the value of gold and silver, as long as they are used as money, depends but slightly, if at all, on the cost of production and on supply and demand. The only effect of the cost of production on the precious metals, is to increase or diminish the number of persons engaged in mining them. When the precious metals cost more to produce than their value as money, they cannot rise in value as long as they can be obtained for consumption by melting coin. And when the cost of producing the precious metals diminishes, they cannot fall below their value as money, because the holders of them can always have them coined and use them as money. Whenever the mining of gold and silver will not procure the same amount of commodities and services that can be ob-

* "Gold and silver, like all other commodities, are valuable only in proportion to the quantity of labor necessary to produce them and bring them to market. Gold is about fifteen times dearer than silver, not because there is a greater demand for it, nor because the supply of silver is fifteen times greater than that of gold, but solely because fifteen times the quantity of labor is necessary to produce a given quantity of it." (Ricardo, Principles of Political Economy, p. 421.)

"If the proportion of either metal alter very materially, as there seems considerable prospect of being the case, from the amazing abundance of the gold fields of California and Australia, their value must alter, just in the same way as a very material alteration in the supply of any other commodity will cause an alteration in its value." (Macleod, Theory and Practice of Banking, vol. i, p. 116.)

tained for a similar amount of labor, capital, and intelligence, employed at other occupations, capital and labor will leave mining for other occupations; and whenever mining will procure more enjoyments than other occupations, capital and labor will quit other occupations to go to mining. But the extent of the possible transfers of labor and capital from other occupations to mining is, and probably always will be, quite limited, for emigration from distant localities to the mining districts, like all emigration, is very difficult and must always be slow and limited in extent, because emigrants can never transfer with themselves, the useful and indispensable results of labor, such as manufactories, houses, streets, roads, canals, railroads, cattle and horses, improvements of arable lands, and other fixtures that form by far the greatest portion of all existing capital. Very productive mines may, however, momentarily, cause a local rise of wages and prices, but the production of the most productive mines will probably ever bear so slight a proportion to the aggregate capital and productions of the world at large, that the value of the latter can never be much, if at all, affected by any future production of gold and silver. The effects, therefore, of even highly productive mines of the precious metals, can probably never be more than local and temporary; and even the local effects of productive mines are kept in check by the very rise of wages and prices they locally produce, as this general rise of prices becomes a powerful inducement to capital and labor to leave mining and go back to other occupations, since a rise of prices increases the productiveness of other occupations while it diminishes that of mining.

The discovery of the gold mines in Australia caused the prices of all things to quadruple in two years, from August 1851 to July 1853. In the subsequent eighteen months, from July 1853 to January 1855, most commodities gradually fell until they touched ruinous prices. Mr. Newmarch says: "The level of wages and the prices of certain kinds of commodities in Melbourne, were reduced to the level prevailing, *cœteris paribus*, in other countries. . . . The fall in the prices of all kinds of imported commodities occurred at an early period, and the low prices have been continued. The fall in house rent occurred about the same early period, and has been more or less continued. No material fall has occurred in 1856, in the large number of articles of food and necessity producible only within the colony. The general result has been, that within a comparatively short period after the establishment of rates of quadrupled wages, the laborers of the colony had the advantage of an exceedingly low range of prices of nearly all imported articles; and of falling prices of all articles of colonial production, the supply of which admitted of comparatively easy extension. . . The effect of the increased supplies of gold in Victoria, in largely increasing the prices of commodities within the colony, was temporary as concerns the most numerous class of commodities."*

In California the effect of the gold mines was very similar. In 1848 and 1849 prices were excessive, whilst in 1851 goods were often not worth their storage.

As to the effects on the value of gold and silver of an increased production of these metals, how can an

* Tooke, History of Prices, vol. vi, pp. 804–812.

increased production affect the value of an article for which the demand is unlimited, and of which, therefore, there can probably never be a glut? On the other hand, how can a diminished supply seriously affect the value of a thing, whose functions can, in a great measure, be performed by other things? That this is the case with gold and silver, is quite evident, for before the introduction of paper money and credit, exchanges were made without coin, by means of barter; and since the introduction of credit and paper money, these ingenious, convenient, and economical means of effecting exchanges, are infinitely more used than coin, and replace it in most of the transactions of commerce.

## CHAPTER IV.

OF the numerous theories of the economists in regard to money, none seem more generally accepted than the theory that gold and silver cannot successfully be used simultaneously as the measure of value, because their relative value varies with the supply and demand, and with the cost of production of these metals. Xenophon said: "As to money, it is the very reverse of all other things. The greater the number of mines discovered and worked, the greater the anxiety of the citizens to become owners of them. It may be objected that gold is at least as useful as silver. I shall not deny this. *I shall only remark that gold, if it became more common than silver, would fall in value, whilst silver would rise in value.*"

Sir William Petty in the 17th century said: "The relative value of gold and silver is modified according as human industry extracts more of one than of the other from the bowels of the earth. Consequently only one at a time should be used as money."

Locke said: "Two metals, as gold and silver, cannot be the measure of commerce both together in any country; because the measure of commerce must be perpetually the same, invariable, and keeping the same proportion of value in all its parts. . . . . One may as well make a measure, v. g. a yard, whose parts lengthen and shrink, as a measure of trade of materials that have not always a settled, invariable value to one another. . . . One metal, therefore, alone can be the money of account and contract, and the measure of commerce in any country." *

Michel Chevalier is the most prominent of the numerous modern advocates of this doctrine. The error of the theory is in taking for granted that governments cannot give a fixed, invariable, relative value to the two precious metals. Against this theory we have the important fact that governments constantly and successfully do regulate the relative value of these metals. *In fact this is the only power governments possess over their value*, for coining them does not give them value, but merely designates the quantity and quality of the metal the coins are made of. What has greatly aided in giving currency to the erroneous theory in question, is the solidarity that exists between all nations connected by the ties of commerce. This causes the relative legal value of the two metals in any one locality, to be affected momentarily by their relative legal value in any other country in whose favor a temporary balance of trade has to be liquidated. What occurred in the United States is a striking proof of the power of governments to establish the relative value of gold and silver, as well as of the effects of having different legal relative values in different countries.

In the United States, the relative value of gold and silver was established in 1792 at 1 to 15, which

* Vol. v, p. 151. London Edition, 1823.

was that then adopted by France and most of the European nations; but when France and the rest of Europe subsequently changed the relative value to 1 to 15½, the United States made no alteration in their coinage. The consequence was, that thereafter, whenever the United States had to liquidate a balance of trade in favor of Europe, it was invariably paid in gold as long as that metal could be obtained at 3⅓ per cent. premium or under, because the ounce of gold that could be obtained in the United States for 15 ounces of silver, had the same value in Europe as 15½ ounces of silver. And when Europe had to liquidate a balance of trade in favor of the United States, it was invariably done with silver, because the 15½ ounces of silver that could be obtained in Europe for one ounce of gold, had the same value in the United States, as $1\frac{1}{30}$ ounce of gold. The attention of Congress being called to these facts, an act was passed in 1834, altering the relative value of gold and silver to 1 to 16. This was committing as great an error as the one it attempted to correct. Instead of adopting the same relative value as in Europe, Congress adopted one that inverted the previous difference in the relative values in Europe and the United States. The new relative value made gold about 3¼ per cent. dearer in the United States than in Europe, and silver 3¼ per cent. dearer in Europe than in the United States. At once the currents of the metals were reversed. Silver alone was thereafter sent from the United States to Europe, in liquidation of all balances of trade, as long as it could be obtained at or under 3 per cent. premium, and gold alone was sent by Europe to liquidate the balances of trade in favor of the United States. Under both relative values, the premium on the cheap metal disappeared whenever there was no adverse balance of trade to liquidate in favor of Europe, as then the legal relative value in the United States alone governed the value of both metals there ; whereas each time a balance of trade in favor of Europe was being liquidated, the premium reappeared. It is very evident that the premiums in both these cases were entirely due to the difference in the legal relative values of the precious metals in Europe and in the United States, and not to any variations in their intrinsic or commercial values.

Precisely the same thing occurred in England in the reign of James I. Gold, being estimated too low at the mint compared with silver, was freely exported, which caused incessant complaints. To remedy this evil, King James raised the value of gold in his coins by successive proclamations ; but he at last raised it too high, and during the remainder of his reign, and that of Charles I, the silver coins were exported until the complaints were as great for want of silver as they had been before for want of gold.*

Sir Isaac Newton, with his usual clear perception of the principles governing phenomena, discovered the cause and pointed out the remedy for the difficulty in the way of using the two metals as standards of value. In his report as master of the mint, he said : "it appears by experience as well as by reason, that silver flows from those places where its value is lowest in proportion to gold, as from Spain to all Europe, and from all Europe to the East Indies, China and Japan,

* Lord Liverpool, Coins of the Realm, p. 118.

and that gold is most plentiful in those places in which its value is highest in proportion to silver, as in Spain and England." He pointed out that it was the irregularity in the valuation of these two metals, that caused so much transmission of one or the other from place to place, "and if gold were lowered only, so as to have the same proportion to the silver money in England, which it hath to silver in the rest of Europe, there would be no temptation to export silver rather than gold to any other part of Europe. And to compass this last, there seems nothing more requisite than to take off about 10*d.* or 12*d.* from the guinea, so that gold may bear the same proportion to the silver money in England, which it ought to do by the course of trade and exchange in Europe."* And yet after quoting this, Macleod says: "their market values (of gold and silver) were constantly varying, and *from causes quite beyond the reach of any law.*" †

The facts cited appear to us to prove conclusively that governments, by common accord, can establish and maintain any given relative value between the two metals, as long as they are used as money.

Another very important fact to notice in regard to the different relative legal values given to gold and silver, is that *it is always the cheap metal that is scarce and the dear metal that is abundant;* the very reverse of what invariably occurs with commodities, which are always cheap where abundant, and dear where scarce; another proof that money does not follow the same laws as commodities.

* Macleod, Theory and Practice of Banking, vol. i, p. 163.

† Theory and Practice of Banking, vol. i, p. 279.

The relative value of gold and silver at different periods has been :

| | |
|---|---|
| In ancient Greece and Rome.................. | 1 to 12 |
| In Greece, after the conquests of Alexander the Great.................................. | 1 to 10 |
| In Italy, after the conquests of Julius Cæsar... | 1 to 9 |
| After the conquest of Sicily by the Romans, where large quantities of silver were found.. | 1 to 17 |
| At the end of the 15th century, in Europe..... | 1 to 11 |
| In England, in 1604........................ | 1 to $12\frac{1}{10}$ |
| In England, in 1626........................ | 1 to $13\frac{1}{3}$ |
| In 1641, in France.......................... | 1 to $13\frac{1}{2}$ |
| In 1641, in Spain........................... | 1 to 14 |
| In England, in 1666........................ | 1 to $14\frac{1}{2}$ |
| In England, in 1717........................ | 1 to $15\frac{1}{5}$ |
| In the middle of the 18th century, in Holland.. | 1 to $14\frac{1}{2}$ |
| In the middle of the 18th century, in France.. | 1 to 15 |

By the act of the 7th Germinal, year 11 (28th March, 1803), France adopted the present relative value of 1 to $15\frac{1}{2}$, which has since become the general relative value in Europe, wherever both the metals are legal tenders.

From 1344 to 1664 a double standard prevailed in England, both silver and gold being a legal tender ; the silver coins at the rate they were issued from the mint, the gold coins at rates fixed, from time to time, by royal proclamation. From 1717 it was declared by proclamation, at the recommendation of Sir Isaac Newton, then master of the mint, that the guinea should be taken as the equivalent of twenty-one shillings in silver. This fixed the relative value at 1 to $15\frac{2859}{13640}$ Both metals continued a legal tender at this relative value till 1774, when silver was disallowed as a legal tender for sums exceeding £25. In 1816 the pound of standard silver was coined into sixty-six shillings, establishing the relative value at 1 to 14.287 ; silver was declared to be a legal tender only for sums of forty shillings or under, and thenceforth it was only coined for account of the Government. The object of this last alteration of the relative value of the precious metals was to prevent the exportation of the silver coins.

In ancient times, alterations in the relative value of the two metals were easily produced by the influx of quite moderate amounts of either, because they were then principally used as commodities, and their value therefore followed the natural laws that govern the value of commodities. But since the 15th century, after commerce took some development, and required large amounts of the precious metals as money, all the alterations in the relative value of the precious metals have been in one uniform direction, up to the influx of gold from California and Australia, viz : the appreciation of gold and the depreciation of silver. This fact is very significant, and explains the cause of these alterations. Gold being the most valuable metal, is much the most convenient to transport and to handle ; and for this convenience, so long as gold did not exist in sufficient quantity to suffice for all transactions, many persons were willing to pay a premium for it rather than be inconvenienced with silver, just as persons constantly pay a premium for a draft on another city or country rather than carry or transmit coin or bank notes. In both these cases the premium paid is a mere remuneration for the services rendered by the convenient coin or draft beyond those that could be rendered by the inconvenient coin. It does not indicate that one is overvalued or undervalued, nor that one will purchase more commodities than the other. It is simply that the holder of the convenient coin or draft will not exchange it for inconvenient coin unless he receives some remuneration for the inconvenience or expense he may incur by the exchange. Premiums of this nature are always exceedingly limited in amount, because the main operations of commerce are invariably made by the most economical means possible. Whenever the premium on a convenient coin is greater than the expense and trouble of handling and transporting the inconvenient coin, commerce performs all its operations with the inconvenient coin rather than pay the premium for the convenient one. But the theorists could not discover this simple reason for the premium on gold in former times, when the supply was inadequate to the demand. They constantly asserted that the premium on gold was an indication that the intrinsic or commercial value of gold had risen, and they urged the governments to alter their legal relative value so as to conform with their intrinsic value. This undoubtedly caused the numerous alterations that took place, each nation increasing the legal value of gold so as to retain it in circulation. But every increase in the relative value of gold still left this metal at a premium. The partisans of the theory that the two metals could not be used simultaneously as legal standards, saw in this constant premium on gold notwithstanding governmental action, proof positive that governments could not regulate their relative value ; whereas the fact is that increasing the value of gold only augments the inducement to pay a premium for it, since it increases the principal advantage gold offers over silver—greater lightness for equal value. Were gold and silver coined at 1 to 30, the premium on the former, as long as the quantity in existence was insufficient for all transactions, would be greater than when coined at 1 to 15, because half the weight of gold would then perform the same service as twice the amount did before, in comparison with silver. As soon as the large production of gold in California and Australia rendered this metal abundant, the premium on it disappeared. Here, again, the theorists claimed a proof of the correctness of their theory ; gold was evidently falling in proportion to silver, as they had predicted ; whereas the disappearance of the premium only indicated that gold had become sufficiently abundant to supply the demand, which was clearly not the case before. In the United States there has been a recent striking example of a similar premium being paid for coin on account of its convenience, irrespective of its intrinsic value. After the exportation of silver had drained that country of its small silver coins, four per cent. premium was paid for the old Spanish rials and half-rials (12½ and 6¼ cent pieces), although the United States mint had ascertained and announced that they were not, on an average, worth within ten per cent. of their nominal value, in consequence of their loss of weight by wear and tear. And exactly as in Europe with gold, the moment United States silver coins became sufficiently abundant to supply all the wants of the community, the premium on the small Spanish coins entirely disappeared.

Sir Isaac Newton had recommended that the guinea,

which passed current at 21*s.* 6*d.*, should be reduced 10*d.* or 12*d.*, which would have made the relative value of gold and silver the same in England as it was on the continent of Europe. His advice was but partially adopted, the guinea being only reduced to twenty-one shillings, which was still too high, and silver consequently continued to be exported in preference to gold. "From 1717 to 1816 no silver coins of legal weight and purity could be retained in circulation, but were exported to foreign countries, where they passed at full value."* What was this full value that attracted silver from England to foreign countries? Not its value elsewhere as a commodity, to be used in the arts, but its legal relative value to gold as money; in other words, the fictitious legal relative value as coin, given it in other countries by governments. How could England retain silver when $15\frac{2859}{13640}$ ounces of it had the same value there as one ounce of gold, whilst on the continent of Europe one ounce of gold had only the same legal value as fifteen ounces of silver? The exportation of silver after the suspension of specie payments by the Bank of England, when the relative legal value on the continent of Europe had become 1 to $15\frac{1}{2}$, was caused by other reasons: by the demand for the precious metals to pay the British armies on the Continent and the subsidies to the Continental powers. This demand was so imperious that the legal value of the precious metals, in either locality, was entirely disregarded.

It was the arguments against the two standards that led Great Britain, in 1774, to adopt gold as the only

* Encyclopædia Britannica, Money.

standard, silver being made a legal tender only for sums of £25 and under. During the French Revolution, the Legislature of France repeatedly discussed the question of the double standard at great length, but finally maintained the double standard, which was very generally used by all European nations except England.

After the discovery of the gold mines of California, Michel Chevalier and the economists in general revived the old theory of the impossibility of maintaining an uniform relative value between the two metals, because, according to them, every increase in the production of either, deranges their relative value. Mr. Chevalier predicted that gold would fall to one half of its present value. The greatest uneasiness prevailed everywhere in consequence of the apprehended fall in the value of gold, and rise in the value of silver. Governments were urged to demonetize gold, and two nations, Holland and Belgium, actually acted on this suggestion and made silver the only legal tender.* Every trifling fluctuation in the value of either metal was immediately accepted by these theorists, without examination or analysis, as proof positive of the realization of their predictions; whereas, when closely analyzed, they all prove that the theory they advanced is completely erroneous.† The following, in addition to long, imposing arrays of figures

* "It became a prevalent belief, that a marked divergence from the previous scale of relative values existing between gold and silver would rapidly manifest itself, and that this divergence would become so decided that sound policy would lead to the substitution of silver for gold as a standard metal in metallic circulations. It was in pursuance of this opinion that Holland demonetized its gold coins." (Tooke, History of Prices, vol. vi, p. 197.)

† The result of the inquiries instituted seems to justify a positive opinion

of the past, present, and future production, existence, and consumption of the two metals, were the facts generally appealed to, to sustain their theories :

1st. The premium paid for gold when scarce, previous to the influx of gold from California and Australia.

2d. The disappearance of the premium on gold after the influx of gold from the Californian and Australian mines.

3d. The discount at which gold bullion and foreign gold coins were sold in 1851 in the United States and in Europe.

4th. The premium formerly paid in the United States on gold, when coined as 1 to 15, and that subsequently paid there on silver, when coined as 1 to 16.

5th. The premium paid for silver in exchange for gold, after 1851.

All these facts, except the 3d, certainly establish some alterations in the value of one or the other of the precious metals ; but when analyzed with care, they are found to maintain our theory, and not that which we combat, for none of these alterations were caused by a change in the cost of production, or in the intrinsic value as commodities of either of these metals. The 1st, 2d, and 4th of these facts have already been fully explained, and certainly indicate no alteration in the

that the fluctuating increase of two or three per cent. in the price of silver, as compared with gold, which has prevailed, at various periods since 1849, admits of being fully explained by circumstances *not* connected with a fall in the value of gold." (Tooke, History of Prices, vol. vi, p. 199.)

natural relative value of the two metals. The discount at which gold bullion and foreign gold coin were sold for a time, was solely caused by the fact that the mints, at that time, were nowhere organized to coin promptly the enormous amounts of gold deposited with them for that purpose; and the discount was a mere allowance to compensate the loss of interest caused by the delay in obtaining the coin from the mints in exchange for the gold deposited. This is clearly proved by the fact that at the very time that uncoined gold was selling at a discount, gold coin was everywhere willingly accepted, at par, in exchange for silver at par. Shortly after uncoined gold ceased to be sold at a discount in Paris, the Bank of France refused to pay out gold except at a premium of 3 per mille, a proof that gold was still generally preferred to silver. Therefore it is evident that the discount on gold bullion and foreign gold coins, was also no indication of an alteration in the natural relative value of the precious metals.

The 5th and last fact, the recent premium on silver in Europe, was the consequence of the large and constant balances of trade which England had to pay to Asia, where silver alone is used as money. England, no longer using silver as a legal tender, had no stock of this metal from which to supply her wants, and therefore had to procure that metal in those countries where there existed a stock of silver, where it was used as a legal tender, as money. But the apprehensions of a fall in gold and a rise in silver, created by the arguments of Michel Chevalier and his partisans, induced the Bank of France and the other large holders of silver, to refuse to exchange silver for gold at par. The

English were thus forced to resort to the money changers of the Continent, who, by paying a slight premium for silver, obtained in exchange for gold, the amounts required by England to liquidate the balances of trade due to Asia. But in 1861, the demand for silver for Asia diminished so much that the premium on this metal disappeared in July of that year, and the Bank of France again paid it out in preference to gold. Previous to this, however, between the 1st of July, 1853, and the 1st of January, 1856, the Bank of France had purchased abroad gold to the amount of 1,363 millions of francs, *for which it paid* 14 *millions of francs as premiums,* say over one per cent., so as to enable it to retain its stock of silver !* and it paid this premium of one per cent. for gold, at the very time this metal was said to be falling in value, and whilst the Bank paid it out at par ! This is one result of attempting to arrest or counteract a natural law ! It must not be forgotten, that at the very moment that the premium on silver disappeared, the relative stock of gold was greater, and that of silver less, than at any time previous while silver was at a premium ; and the production of gold was then greater than at any previous moment. It is, therefore, very evident that the premium on silver, also, was no proof of any change in the natural relative value of the precious metals. That the premium on silver was entirely due to the demand for Asia, is not only proved by the fact that the premium disappeared as soon as the demand for Asia diminished, but also by the following statistics :

The exportations of silver from France from 1852 to

* M. Chevalier, De la baisse probable de l'or, p. 42.

1859, inclusive, *exceeded* the importations by frs. 1,378,862,000 ($275,750,000). The *total exportations* of silver from France during the same period being frs. 2,505,813,178;* whilst the exportations of silver from England and the Mediterranean ports, for China and the East Indies, during those years, were frs. 1,917,500,000,† say 76½ per cent. of the entire exports from France. If we take only the years 1856 to 1859, inclusive, the exportations of silver from England and the Mediterranean ports for China and the East Indies, amount to 93 per cent. of the entire export of silver from France in those years. Mr. Chevalier himself admits "that the value of silver has risen at present, because the demand for the metal has been suddenly increased for a special destination, for exportation to Asia." ‡

The large exportation of silver from France, where it was worth a premium, toward Asia where it only circulates at its former value, is another conclusive proof that the premium paid for silver was not caused by an increase in the intrinsic or natural value of silver; and also, that the value of the precious metals is not governed by the same natural laws that govern the value of other things. If the same laws controlled the value of gold and silver, that control the value of commodities, how could such large exportations from France, of a

* Revue Contemporaine, 15 Mars, 1860, p. 12.

† Circular of Mr. Low, of London, January 1, 1861.

‡ De la baisse probable de l'or, p. 59. "It will be found that the variations in the price of silver follow the variations in the shipments of silver to the East. . . . We find that the rise in the price of silver is manifestly connected with the large and extraordinary demand for silver as an article of remittance to India and China in payment for commodities." (Tooke History of Prices, vol. vi, pp. 675, 676.)

metal that country does not produce, have caused so slight a variation in its value as that which has occurred? Mr. Chevalier himself admits that "at this moment the depreciation of gold in comparison to silver is very small. . . . It is even remarkable that the fall in gold, as compared with silver, has been thus far almost imperceptible. In this respect, all the anticipations which appeared most certain have experienced a postponement which, at first sight, would appear to overthrow the theory, but which however is not inexplicable."* The only explanation, however, given by Mr. Chevalier, of the non-fulfilment of his predictions, is that France, by permitting the exchange of her silver for gold, has been a parachute to retard the fall of gold! How could the premium on silver be maintained after the liquidation of the balance of trade in favor of Asia? Certainly not from a demand for coinage from England, Switzerland, Belgium, Portugal, Spain, Russia, Brazil, or the United States, for in all these countries gold is a legal tender, and facilitates the exchanges of commodities better than silver, which, in most of these countries, is now a legal tender for small amounts only, being only coined to a limited amount exclusively for government account, at a higher value than its legal value in France. Certainly not from the demand for consumption in the arts, for the annual production of the silver mines greatly exceeds the demand for that purpose.

The British Government evidently committed a great error in not encouraging the circulation of gold in India. Instead of doing this, the East India Company, apparently from fear of the impending fall in the value of

* De la baisse probable de l'or, p. 228.

gold predicted by Mr. Chevalier, sent instructions to India to refuse, in payment of taxes, the gold mohurs which had been hitherto received, and, to accept nothing but silver.* If the East India Company, instead of discouraging the circulation of gold, had coined the metal in India, and made it a legal tender there, this convenient metal would, probably, not only have been introduced into general circulation in India, but also eventually into China, owing to the constant intercourse between those countries. In that event, instead of transporting, as now, the greater part of the production of the Australian mines to England, to be thence taken to the continent of Europe, where it is exchanged for silver at a premium, which silver is then carried to India, the gold of Australia would go direct to India and China, thereby saving heavy expenses and loss of interest, whilst Europe would not feel alarm at the prospect of losing her silver.

* "A gold coin was introduced, 1st September, 1835, called a 'mohur,' equal to fifteen rupees, worth 1*l.* 9*s.* 2*d.* Previous to 1st September, 1835, gold as well as silver was a legal tender in India; but under the law of 1835, silver was adopted as the exclusive standard. In 1841, however, the Indian Government found it expedient to authorize their collectors to receive gold mohurs whenever tendered. But in December, 1852, a public notification was issued, that gold coins would be no longer received by the public officers. The effect of this modification, which is still in force, is again to render *silver* the single standard metal in India. The origin of the change of December, 1852, is said to have been a somewhat sudden increase in the quantity of gold coin tendered by the public, and an apprehension, on the part of the Government, that they might possibly be led into the predicament of having to accept all payments made to them in gold as the cheapest metal, and to make all payments to others in *silver*, the dearer metal, and the only legal tender. The question is an intricate one; but it seems probable that the notification of December, 1852, *was somewhat hastily adopted.*" (Tooke, History of Prices, Vol. vi, pp. 722, 723.)

## CHAPTER V.

It is evident that the advent of gold could not increase the value of silver. Both metals being used for the same purpose, and gold being the most convenient, and, therefore, generally preferred, as soon as the stock of gold sufficed for all the wants of the community, silver would have been less used than formerly, and consequently would have fallen in value, were it not a legal tender. In any event, both metals being principally used as money, as instruments of exchanges, gold could not fall in value in consequence of an increased production, without producing a corresponding fall in the value of silver, as long as both metals were used as money, at their former relative legal value. It is surprising that so eminent an economist as Mr. Chevaliër should have failed to perceive that if a redundancy of money depreciates its exchangeable value, the depreciation will affect equally all the currencies that are current in the community, no matter which may be the one that is increased in quantity. In a community where gold, silver, and convertible bank notes circulate, it is perfectly immaterial which of these currencies is increased. If gold, from over supply, should diminish in value, silver and bank notes would experience the same depreciation, although the quantity of the latter currencies in circulation be not increased, nay, even if they were diminished, for if the volume of the currency affects its value, it must be the aggregate amount, and not the amount of any one of the several currencies, that must regulate its value. In all communities where several currencies exist, the one least desired or most easily or economically obtained, is invariably most used, and thus maintains its value and prevents the rise of the other currencies.

All variations in the value of mixed currencies, as long as they all remain a legal tender or are willingly accepted, is expressed or shown by a premium on the preferred, and not by a discount on the less desired currency.

Mr. Chevalier, whilst advocating the adoption by all European nations of silver as the standard, denies that he desires to have gold abandoned as money. He proposes that gold should be coined, by stamping on the coins the weight and fineness of the metal they contain, and that they should then be received and paid by the community, either at their daily value at the several exchanges, measured by silver, or at the value that governments should, periodically, establish. Had he reflected that nothing that fluctuates constantly in nominal value can properly perform the functions of money, he would have perceived that this idea was impracticable, and would simply result in the demonetization of gold, to the great inconvenience of all communities, as they would thus lose the use of the most convenient metallic currency. The withdrawal of gold from circulation could not fail to create serious disturbances in the operations of commerce and industry, for the value of all things would then have to be measured, and all exchanges would have to be carried on with one metal alone, silver, the stock of which is evidently insufficient for all the requirements of the world. Holland attempted to use gold coins having no fixed value, and the result was, as we predicted before the experiment was made, that after about 200,000 florins had been coined, the demand ceased entirely! Michel Chevalier acknowledges that commerce, *in consequence of their uncertain value*, makes little use in Holland of these new gold coins." * Germany made the same experiment, with similar results.†

Everything indicates that the advantages of the demonetization of gold are purely imaginary. The main argument for demonetizing gold is that the large production of this metal at present will reduce its value. But will its demonetization prevent the fall of gold if it must take place? Evidently not; on the contrary it would hasten and increase the fall greatly, for the enormous amount now used as coin would then all be offered for consumption as a commodity, and as the yearly consumption in the arts is at present but a small portion of the annual production of the mines, gold

* De la baisse probable de l'or, p. 89.

† "Holland and Germany attempted to retain gold in circulation without giving it a fixed value. In one case the value was to be settled by the parties in interest when used; in the other it was to pass current at rates to be announced every six months by the governments. But these states do not appear to have succeeded in retaining in circulation an amount of gold worth mentioning." (E. de Parieu, Revue Contemporaine of Paris, 15th March, 1860, p. 13.)

"In Holland and in Belgium, gold continues to circulate, but simply as a commodity whose value is daily adjusted by commerce, and *consequently it is but little used.*" (Michel Chevalier, De la baisse probable de l'or, p. 89.)

would have to fall, not only to a price that would arrest all further production for the present, but even to one so much below the cost of production as to tempt capitalists to purchase and store it until needed for consumption. Imagine the fall that would have to take place to induce capitalists to purchase a commodity that might remain on their hands twenty, thirty, or forty years, according as the demand might be stimulated by the reduction of price!

Mr. Chevalier says that if the plan be adopted of regulating the value of gold by periodical government edicts, the individual members of the community need only hold, at those periods, such amount of gold as they chose! * How could this be done? All that exists must be held by somebody. What one sells, another must buy. And by attempting to sell at the approach of those periods, the fall in value would probably exceed the depreciatiou that would be announced by the government edict, so that instead of escaping the loss by selling the gold before these periods, it is probable it would only aggravate it.

The production of the two metals was formerly 1 oz. of gold to 46 oz. of silver; whereas in 1853 it was 1 oz. of gold to 4 oz. of silver; and yet no fluctuations in value exceeding 3 or 4 per cent. have ever taken place since this great change in the relative production of the precious metals; † and all these fluctuations were clearly caused by other reasons than a change in the value

* De la baisse probable de l'or, p. 235.

† "The production of gold from 1800 to 1848 was equal to fifty-eight per cent. of the total stock in 1800, without affecting, in any way that can be discovered, the relative value of gold." (Tooke, History of Prices, vol. vi, p. 232.)

of gold as a commodity. If so great an alteration in the relative production of the two metals has produced no alteration in their relative value, is it probable that any future alteration in their production can produce any effect so long as both metals continue to be principally used as money?

Belgium demonetized gold, but readopted it in 1861, making both metals once more a legal tender, at the urgent and reiterated requests of her commercial and industrial interests, and in defiance of the opinion of the theorists. The fact is, the advantages of the double standard are so great, that all the countries that use gold as the only legal standard, invariably coin silver, slightly debased, and make it a legal tender for limited amounts. The discarded metal thus still forms a more or less considerable portion of the currency. In England, for example, the silver in circulation forms a fifth or a sixth of the whole metallic currency.* Is not this currency given to silver where gold alone is made the legal standard, an ample acknowledgment of the superiority of the double standard? The act of 1844 authorizes the Bank of England to hold in the issue department silver to the extent of one fourth of the amount of gold bullion and coin held at any particular time. Sir Robert Peel, in presenting the bill of 1844, said that a certain portion of the bank issues would be allowed to be on silver bullion, "as the export of silver bullion was a proper remedy for *the in-*

* "The amount of gold in circulation in Great Britain, *including that in the Bank of England*, is variously estimated at from forty-four to sixty millions sterling. The silver is estimated at £11,000,000, but that includes the coin in the colonies." (Gilbart on Banking.)

*convenience of our standard differing from that of other nations.* It was therefore of great importance to insure such a stock of silver in this country as might meet the wants of merchants and *prevent their having to send to the Continent for it.*" * The committee of the House of Lords of 1847 recommended that the act of 1844 be amended so that the issues of bank notes on silver might be extended."† John Horsley Palmer, Esq., then a director of the Bank of England, in 1848 testified before a committee of the House of Commons that one of his objections to the bank act of 1844, "is the limitation of the quantity of silver bullion permitted to be held in the issue department: seeing that silver is equally available with gold for foreign payments, a portion of that restriction might, with perfect safety, be withdrawn, and thereby greater facilities afforded in meeting an unfavorable exchange." J. Pease, Esq., testified before the same committee that he paid wages to the extent of £10,000 to £15,000 per month, and added, "I should like to see silver a legal tender to a larger amount—£200, or at least £100." Mr. Thomas Baring said, in a speech in Parliament in 1848, "I know an instance in 1847 where it was found impossible to raise a penny upon £60,000 worth of silver, a precious metal, a legal tender in most parts of the civilized world. It was not a question of price with the bank, but a question affecting its own safety. The bank could only issue notes on silver to the extent of one fifth of the bullion in the bank, and as they had

* Macleod, Theory and Practice of Banking, vol. ii, p. 297.

† Tooke, History of Prices, vol. v, p. 492.

not a sufficient amount of gold to be within this limitation, they could not purchase the silver." *

It is self-evident that there are great disadvantages in the adoption by different countries of different metals as the legal standard. How could France, were she to adopt silver as the only legal standard, liquidate a balance of trade in favor of England, where gold alone is a legal tender? And how could England then liquidate a balance of trade in favor of France? Such a state of things would render the legal money of both countries useless as means of liquidating balances of trade in favor of the other, and yet this is one of the most important functions of coin at the present day. And this would be compensated by no advantage, for the resort to a single standard cannot prevent the exportation of the metal used as the standard, whenever it is required in other countries; it only adds to the inconvenience produced by the exportation, as the metal exported cannot be replaced by the other, as when the the double standard is used.† When England has to pay silver to Asia, where can England obtain it, except in the countries where it exists in abundance? and that is, invariably, the countries where it is used as a

* Alison's History of Europe, vol. viii, p. 101, American edition.

† "Belgium, as is well known, has demonetized gold: the measure was a good one (!!), and yet that country has also suffered from the exportation of its silver coin." (R. de Fontenay, Journal des Economistes, June, 1860, p. 396.)

"Germany, that uses silver almost exclusively, has found it very difficult to prevent the exportation to England, via Hamburg, of this sole metallic circulation." (E. de Parieu, Revue Contemporaine, 15th March, 1860, p. 14.)

legal tender; for to those countries alone, where it is a legal tender at its full value, does either metal flow.

As each of the precious metals offers peculiar advantages for special purposes, it is the interest of all nations that both should be universally coined and used as legal tenders. Why should governments refuse to render the service of certifying the quantity and quality of either of the precious metals, which is all they do by coining them, merely because it may be at a premium for exportation? Does not the foreign trade merit assistance and protection as well as the home trade? If a premium on a metal be a sufficient reason to cease to coin it, the owners of the bullion will cease to carry it to the mint to be coined. But it is absurd to enact a law forbidding the state from rendering this service, when the owners of the bullion request it, whatever be the use they may afterward make of the coin.

To-day there is more danger, despite all the arguments of Michel Chevalier and his partisans, that silver will be universally demonetized than gold, for already Russia, Portugal, and Chili have followed the example of England, making gold the only legal standard. In Switzerland and the United States, both gold and silver are yet a legal tender, but the fractions of the dollar in the United States, and the coins under 5 francs in Switzerland, are only a legal tender for limited amounts, being slightly debased, and coined solely for account of the government. There can be no serious objections to the system adopted by the United States and Switzerland, if the debased coins were redeemed by the governments that issue them, whenever presented for that purpose, so as to prevent over issues. This should also be done in regard to all copper and nickel coins, which are generally issued by the mints at a much higher value than that of the metal they contain.

Mr. Chevalier says the exchange of silver at a premium for gold at par is a disastrous exchange for France! * How so? Does a country ever export what is needful to the well-being of its own inhabitants? The fact that a product or a precious metal is exported in exchange for something else, is proof positive that both parties to the exchange are benefited thereby, for otherwise the exchange would not be made. Every commercial operation is made because it is supposed to be advantageous by both seller and buyer. All commercial transactions, freely repeated, must be advantageous to the individuals making them, and, consequently, to the nations of which they are citizens; for the prosperity of a nation depends entirely on the prosperity of the individuals composing the nation. The idea that there can be a national interest distinct from individual interest, is a legacy of the olden times, which political economy is slowly destroying; but unfortunately the error yet exists in the minds of many considered intelligent and enlightened!

Mr. de Parieu also says that the community in France suffers from the exchange of silver at a premium for gold at par; and yet he subsequently acknowledges that the gold received renders the same services as the silver given in exchange.† Furthermore, he asserts that the scarcity of silver has induced the counterfeiting of silver coins! ‡ But he admits, subsequently,

* De la baisse probable de l'or, p. 190.

† Revue Contemporaine, 16th March, 1860, p. 14. ‡ Ib., p. 15.

he has also heard of some cases of counterfeiting the gold coins.* He asserts that the exportation of silver from France is the consequence of the rise in value of that metal; † whereas, evidently, the rise in the value of silver is the consequence of the demand for that metal for exportation, for the moment that demand ceased, silver fell to its former value.

Mr. de Parieu quotes the following extract from a report of the Federal Council of Switzerland: "There yet remains in France about 1,000 millions of silver, and if the French Government does not delay too long, it may secure for its own benefit the profit which speculators will otherwise obtain." ‡ But to whom does this silver belong? to the government, or to the individual holders? If to the latter, why should they not profit by the rise in its value, if there be any? By what right can the government claim it?

Mr. de Fontenay says, silver is the preferable standard, because it cannot vary in value as much as gold, as the cost of production of silver is greater than that of gold. § Is not the talented editor of Bastiat's works advancing here the very doctrine so admirably and so wittily refuted by Bastiat in his Sophismes Economiques, "that fertility is injurious—that abundance and cheapness are disadvantageous—scarcity and dearness desirable"?

Had France, when gold was scarce and at a premium, attempted to introduce it largely into her circulation by increasing its legal value, she would have lost

* Revue Contemporaine, 16th March, 1860, p. 16.
† Journal des Economistes, April, 1860, p. 1.
‡ Ib., p. 16.
§ Ib., June, 1860, p. 398.

the premium she would have had to pay for the gold, at the same time that she would have driven to other countries, as was the case with the United States, the silver she has since sold at a premium in exchange for gold at par. We have here an evidence of the advantages to be derived by allowing things to take their natural course, without interference from human laws and regulations.

From what precedes it follows:

1st. That money is the measure of the relative value, or rather the common denominator of the value, of all things except itself.

2d. That the value of money can only be measured by its exchange for other things. It is just as impossible to measure the value of money by money itself, or by the bullion of which it is made, as to measure the value of a bushel of wheat by another bushel of the same wheat, or to ascertain the value of a fraction of which the denominator alone is given. *

3d. That if money cannot measure the value of money, it is just as impossible to measure the value of gold coin by silver coin, or *vice versa*, so long as they are both a legal tender, as to measure the value of a bushel of wheat by the value of two half bushels of the same wheat.

* "When the coin is of full weight, and the mint charges nothing for coinage, coin and bullion must be of precisely equal value, and cannot measure one another. We might as well talk of the weight of water in water, or of the value of lead in lead, as of the price of gold in gold. Were an ounce of gold to fall one tenth of its present cost of production, or to cost ten times as much labor as it does now, still, while the regulations of the mint are unaltered, it will be worth 3*l.* 17*s.* 10½*d.*" (Edinburgh Review, Ootober, 1846, p. 89.)

4th. That the relative value of the precious metals, as long as used as money, depends entirely on the relative value at which governments make them a legal tender; but this *legal* relative value in one country affects their relative *market* value in another country, when there is a balance of trade to be liquidated in coin, and the relative legal value is not uniform in both countries. If the difference in the relative legal value of the two metals in two countries be sufficiently large, it may even cause one to be exported without regard to the balance of trade, in which case one metal would constantly be worth more than its legal value in the country where it was valued lowest.

The true and only effectual remedy for all variations in the relative value of gold and silver would be a congress of all the commercial nations, to adopt one uniform relative value for the two metals, both of which should be used everywhere as legal tenders, for it cannot be doubted that two useful instruments are preferable to one. Once establish everywhere a uniform relative value between gold and silver, and make them both a legal tender in all commercial countries, and immediately all variations in their relative value will disappear, because either metal will then liquidate equally well a balance of trade at any point. Gold, being the most convenient to transport, will be generally preferred for foreign payments, and, consequently, without debasing them, there will be no tendency to export the smaller silver coins indispensable to the convenience of local exchanges. The same congress might also adopt some universal system of coinage that would prevent the present needless expense of recoining foreign coins when received in liquidation of balances of trade. This desirable object can be far more readily attained than is generally supposed. In Spain, in Mexico, and in all the republics of South America, accounts are kept in dollars varying little or not at all from the milrés in which accounts are kept in Brazil and Portugal, and from the rix-thalers in which they are kept in Denmark and Sweden. The Austrian, Saxon, and Lubec rix-thalers, as well as the Roman, Venetian, and Sicilian scudos, and the Parma ducat, all have nearly the same value as the Spanish dollars. In France, Belgium, Switzerland and Sardinia, accounts are kept in francs of a perfectly uniform value, and in England in pounds sterling, represented by the sovereign. There is at present but a very trifling difference in the value of a sovereign, 5 dollars, milrés, rix-thalers, scudos, or ducats, and 25 francs. If the different nations would only agree that, hereafter, 25 francs, 5 dollars, milrés, rix-thalers, scudos, or ducats, and a sovereign, should contain precisely the same quantity of fine gold, or a relative quantity of fine silver, at the relative value of the two metals which shall be fixed by the congress, these several coins or moneys, and their several fractions, could thereafter be made a legal tender everywhere, and they would all form a round sum in the money of every other country; so that with the exception of Russia, some portions of Germany, and possibly some portions of Italy, all civilized nations might retain the present denominations of their coins, and yet have them form a portion of a universal currency. The advantage of retaining the coins and denominations in use at present, cannot be overestimated, for nothing is more difficult than to change long-established usages or habits. Some portions of Germany, and possibly of Italy, would have to change their present coins, but in these cases the change would not be very difficult, because the French coins are well known, and already circulate freely in every portion of those countries. In Russia, the change would be more radical and more difficult, but as the present system of money in Russia is quite complicated by different issues of roubles, each having a different value, besides a legal paper currency constantly varying in value, the change, if once made, would undoubtedly simplify the currency, and be much for the better in every respect. The new system could be made entirely decimal, if England would merely modify some of her small coins, and the present complicated calculations required to reduce the currency of one country into that of any other, would then become quite simple and easy.

The proposed system will be clearly understood in all its details by the following table, which shows what would be the value of each coin now in use, in the currency of all the other countries :

Under the proposed system,

| In England. | | | In the United States, Spain, Portugal, &c. | | In France, Belgium, &c. |
|---|---|---|---|---|---|
| The sovereign or 20 shillings, | would be equal | to | $5.00 | or | frs. 25.00 |
| 16 " | " | " | 4.00 | " | 20.00 |
| 10 " | " | " | 2.50 | " | 12.50 |
| 8 " | " | " | 2.00 | " | 10.00 |
| 4 " | " | " | 1.00 | " | 5.00 |
| 2 " | " | " | 0.50 | " | 2.50 |
| 1 " | " | " | 0.25 | " | 1.25 |
| 10 pence | " | " | 0.20 | " | 1.00 |
| 5 " | " | " | 0.10 | " | 0.50 |
| 2½ " | " | " | 0.05 | " | 0.25 |
| 1 penny | " | " | 0.02 | " | 0.10 |
| ½ " | " | " | 0.01 | " | 0.05 |

## CHAPTER VI.

### PAPER MONEY.

RICARDO said that money in its most perfect state, is paper money, and he undoubtedly is perfectly right in this assertion. Paper money is preferable to any other because it is lighter, more easily handled, counted, and transported, than any other money ever used, at the same time that it offers the great additional advantage of being the cheapest material out of which an instrument to facilitate the exchanges of commodities and services can be made. Adam Smith said: "The substitution of paper in the room of gold and silver money, replaces a very expensive instrument of commerce with one much less costly and sometimes equally convenient. Circulation comes to be carried on by a new wheel, which it costs less both to erect and to maintain than the old one." * Another eminent writer on money said: "In proportion as the instruments of commerce or the machinery of manufactures are of a less expensive construction, the articles which they contribute to produce may be afforded at a lower rate. To employ paper money instead of gold, is to substitute a

* Wealth of Nations, vol. ii, p. 25; London edition, 1819.

very cheap instrument of commerce in the room of an expensive one." *

The great and only difficulty in regard to paper money, is the abuses and errors which have attended its use.† But is this a valid reason for refusing, as many desire and propose, to use a great and beneficial instrument of human progress and well being? Is not everything used by man, including his own faculties, susceptible of being abused? Water, fire, food, education, amusements, all things that contribute to the welfare of humanity when properly used, also produce suffering when improperly used. Suffering is a valid reason for ceasing the improper use of anything, but not for ceasing its use altogether. The great aim of man must be to discover the proper and beneficial use of all things. With paper money, as with everything else, the great point is to ascertain clearly what is its proper, and what its improper, use. To this end it is necessary to refer to the experience of the past, and to submit to a close and careful analysis all the facts we can discover bearing on the question—sole means of knowledge within man's reach in this world. With that view, we shall begin by recalling briefly the results of a few of the experiments in regard to government issues of paper money.

The French Government, on the 2d May, 1716, during the regency of the Duke of Orleans, authorized

* Quoted in Rees' Encyclopædia, Paper Currency.

† "If there were perfect security that the power of issuing paper money would not be abused, that is, if there were perfect security for its being issued in such quantities as to preserve its value relatively to the mass of circulating commodities nearly equal, the precious metals might be entirely dispensed with, not only as a circulating medium, but also as a standard to which to refer the value of paper." (McCulloch, Money.)

the celebrated Law to establish a bank with a capital of 6,000,000 livres. Its notes were, by royal edict, made receivable in payment of taxes, and, by a subsequent edict, the tax receivers were even ordered to redeem them in specie on presentation. This at once gave them such currency that the circulation of the bank soon reached 50 millions of livres. The deposits of gold and silver in exchange for bank notes increased every day. In less than two years, Law completely introduced bank notes into circulation in France, where before they had been entirely unknown.

Law's object was, finally, to establish a national bank that should collect the entire public revenue, in the place of the "Fermiers Generaux," and administer all the commercial privileges that might be granted to it by the Government. The emission of bank notes to the extent of ten times the capital of the bank was, in his eyes, too limited a result. He conceived the idea of uniting all the capitalists of France, so as to control all the elements of national wealth, from the landed estates to the colonial trade. What security could be more ample than the whole of France? But Law did not dare to present this project in all its majestic simplicity. Public opinion would not, as yet, permit it. He was forced to graft his national bank on some institution that would accord with the prejudices of his contemporaries; and, unfortunately, the then prevailing mania for colonization furnished him the opportunity to establish a company to trade to the Mississippi. This led to the organization of the "Compagnie des Indes Occidentales" (West India Company), in August, 1717, as an adjunct to Law's bank, with a capital of one hundred millions of livres ; and, as an inducement to subscribe to the shares, they were authorized to be paid for, one fourth in coin and three fourths in "billets d'état" (state notes), which were then greatly depreciated. The West India Company received the grant of the sovereignty and exclusive trade of Louisiana, and the monopoly of the Canada fur trade.

But the main cause of the final catastrophe was, that on the 4th December, 1718, two and a half years after its creation, Law's bank was declared the Royal Bank of France ; the Government guaranteed the notes issued by Law's bank, and reimbursed the old shareholders in coin ; and for all payments above six hundred livres, gold and bank notes alone were declared a legal tender. It thus ceased to be a private enterprise, managed and controlled by the vigilant motive of self-interest, and became exclusively an engine of the state. To the West India Company was further granted, on the 4th September, 1718, the tobacco monopoly ; on the 20th July, 1719, the administration of the mint ; and in May, 1719, all the privileges and trade of the several maritime companies (the China, the Senegal, and the East India companies) were transferred to it, and it assumed the name of the "Compagnie des Indes."

In consequence of these successive annexations, besides its issues of bank notes, the company was forced to issue sundry series of shares. The number of shares —originally 200,000 of 500 livres each—was augmented in May, 1719, by an issue of 50,000 new shares, known as "the daughters," and by a second issue of 50,000 in July, 1719, known as "the granddaughters." A few months later, after the lease of the "fermes" (taxes) had been granted to the company, and it had promised to loan 1,500 millions of livres to the state, four other emissions were made, which carried the total number of shares to 624,000. The rage for them was so great that their price rose from par (500 livres) up to 18,000 livres per share! On the other hand the issues of bank notes, which, by the edicts authorizing them, were to be limited to 1,200 millions—amount about equal to the specie in the kingdom—were admitted by the Government to have been carried to 2,700 millions; and, according to general opinion, the amount issued was really 3,000 millions of livres!

To encourage the circulation of the bank notes, in December, 1719, an edict ordered that, thereafter, they should always be worth five per cent. more than specie! that silver should only be used in payments under 100 livres, and gold in those under 300 livres. To check the growing desire to purchase jewelry and precious stones, as means of obtaining something of intrinsic value in exchange for the bank notes, in which confidence was declining, it was forbidden to wear pearls, diamonds, and other precious stones. The transportation of specie was prohibited between towns in which there were branches of the bank. By edicts of the 23d and 25th February, 1720, it was made obligatory to use bank notes in all payments over 100 livres. No person was permitted to hold more than 500 livres in specie, under penalty of confiscation and a fine of 10,000 livres; and informers were to receive one half of all amounts confiscated. The use of the precious metals for objects of art or luxury, was regulated and limited, so as to prevent an evasion of the limitation of the amount of gold and silver that might be in the possession of any one person. Finally, an edict of 11th March, 1720, forbade any payment being made in specie.

As it was feared that the fall in the price of the shares of the India Company might increase the discredit of the bank notes, it was decreed on the 5th March that the price of the shares should be thereafter 9,000 livres, and an office was opened in the bank, where the shares could be exchanged for bank notes, or bank notes converted into shares, at that price. This decree, instead of benefiting the bank notes, caused a rapid depreciation of their market value. In February they were worth ninety per cent., but after the 5th March only sixty to fifty.

On the 21st May, 1720, an edict reduced the value of the shares to 8,000 livres ; and ordered that on the 1st July it should be further reduced to 7,500 livres, and should thereafter be reduced monthly 500 francs, until the 1st December, when their value would become 5,000 francs, which thereafter was to be their permanent value. The bank notes were only to pass current at eighty per cent. of their par value until the 1st of July, when they were to be reduced to seventy-five per cent., and thereafter further reduced 5 per cent. every month, until the 1st December, when they were to be current at fifty per cent., which was thereafter to be their permanent value. From that moment the whole paper fabric fell to the ground ; the notes lost all credit, none would meddle with them ; on the 22d May any one might have starved with a hundred millions of paper money in his pocket. The edict created such excitement among all classes that the Regent revoked the edict on the 27th May. But all confidence being now gone, this revocation had no other effect than to increase the mischief, by throwing again into the channels of commerce notes universally discredited, with which knavish persons paid and ruined their lawful creditors. To render matters worse, payments were the same day stopped at the bank, commissioners being sent to seal up the vaults and examine the books, under the pretext of inquiring into frauds alleged to have been committed by the clerks, but in reality to prevent the specie from being paid away in exchange for notes.

When the bank thus stopped payment, the circulation was 2,235,085,590 livres, and the specie in its vaults 336,011,050 livres. On the 10th June the bank was opened for the payment of notes of ten livres. On the 11th it was announced that the notes of 100 livres would be changed into small notes, but only one for each person, and the 12th and 13th were appointed for the payment of the notes of ten livres. This drew together an immense number of persons, who were with difficulty controlled by the troops. The 17th July was appointed for the payment of the notes of 100 livres, on which day so extraordinary a concourse of people assembled, and the struggles to reach the bank were such, that it is said no less than twenty persons were suffocated. On the 30th July an edict doubled the legal value of gold and silver, which, however, was to be gradually reduced again, month by month, to their former legal values, the object being, by the temptation of a temporary high value, to induce the holders of coin to put it into circulation, but the edict failed in attaining this object.

In June, 1720, twenty-five millions of livres of perpetual annuities, bearing interest at two and a half per cent. per annum, and four millions of annuities on lives, bearing interest at four per cent. per annum, were created to redeem the bank notes. In July six hundred millions of rentes, and in August eight millions more of perpetual annuities, bearing interest at two and a half per cent. per annum, were created for the same purpose. The terms offered were considered very onerous, and the people did not subscribe to them as rapidly as desired. An edict was therefore issued on the 15th August, declaring that the notes of 10,000 and of 1,000 livres should no longer circulate, except in payment of the annuities and rentes; and, by a subsequent edict, all payments in notes were prohibited after the 1st November, 1720. The consequence was that, many persons having neglected the opportunities of funding their bank notes within the limited time, large amounts proved a total loss.

With regard to the shares, by an edict of 3d of June, 1720, 100,000 belonging to the king, and 300,000 in the hands of the company were cancelled; 200,000 new shares were created and issued in exchange for old shares, share for share, against a payment of 3,000 livres on each share, or two new shares for three old shares; the dividend on the new shares was fixed at 360 francs. Soon afterward 50,000 additional new shares were issued on the same conditions. The farm of the taxes, the mint, and the royal revenues were taken from the company, which thus became a mere trading company. On the 24th of October, an edict directed a list to be made out of all the original proprietors of shares. Those who possessed the full number subscribed for, were ordered to deposit them with the company—those who had either sold the whole or part, were to recomplete their original number by purchasing from the company the deficient shares at 13,500 livres per share. As many persons upon this attempted to leave the country with their property, on the 29th of October, all persons were prohibited, under pain of death, from quitting the kingdom without express permission of the regent.

These operations concluded, it was found that the total amount of the public debt on the 1st of January, 1721, was 2,289,762,849 livres, besides 125,024 shares of the India Company, valued at 899,638,855 livres, making a total of 3,189,401,705 livres, the annual interest on which was 99,588,375 livres.

The ministry, finding it impossible for the nation to sustain, for any length of time, so heavy a charge, issued an edict, dated 26th of January, 1721, appointing a commissioner to take an account of the claims of the state creditors, which were to be divided into five classes; the first four classes were to be composed of those who had acquired their claims by money paid to the king when he discharged the old debt of the state, by the sale of heritable and movable property, and by the disposal of merchandise or other effects, while the fifth and last class were to comprehend all who could give no fair or satisfactory account of the origin of their claims. Deductions at different rates, proportioned to the favorable or unfavorable circumstances attending the claims, were ordered to be made from the first four classes, except claims of or under 500 livres, which were to be paid in full. Those of the fifth class were ordered to be totally cancelled.

The claims deposited under this decree represented 2,222,597,491 livres, which were reduced by the commissioner to 1,676,501,831 livres. The shares were reduced from 125,024 to 56,000, and the dividends on them were reduced from 360 to 100 livres per share for the first ensuing year, and 150 livres thereafter, exclusive of their proportion of the profits of the trade of the company. The expenses of the commission were 9,045,875 livres. The notes at the time of the suspension of the bank had fallen to 80 per cent. discount, and on the 12th of February, 1721, they were only worth 4 per cent. Thus ended the bank and the Compaigne des Indes.*

Our second illustration of government paper issues is also taken from the history of France.

The National Assembly of France decreed, on the 1st of April, 1790, the emission of assignats, based on and in anticipation of the sale of the confiscated landed estates of the emigrant nobles and clergy, in payment of which they were to be received.

The first issue was of 400 millions of francs, but others followed rapidly, and they soon began to depreciate in value. The Government resorted to the most violent and despotic measures to sustain the value of the assignats, such as prohibiting the use of metallic coin; establishing maximum prices for commodities; inflicting severe penalties on all who paid or received them at less

* Thier's Life of Law. Wood's Life of Law, Edinburgh, 1824.

than their par value ; and in 1796 even death was decreed against all who should refuse to receive assignats at par. But all in vain. These measures were powerless to arrest the depreciation. There was a temporary reaction in 1793, when, by means of a forced loan, 840 millions were redeemed, cancelled, and burnt ; but in 1795 the Government made another forced loan, in payment of which the assignats were only received at one per cent. of their nominal value ! How could they continue to circulate as money, when the very Government that had issued them refused them in payment of loans and taxes ? Further large issues were however made ; they soon fell to one half of one per cent., and finally, in the beginning of 1796, to zero. Toward the end, 8,000 to 10,000 francs were paid for a pair of boots ; 600 to 700 francs for a pound of butter, and 20 to 30 francs for a stick of barley sugar !

In 1796 the assignats were withdrawn and redeemed at $\frac{1}{30}$th of their nominal value, with "mandats," which entitled the holder to take possession of public lands at their estimated value, whilst the assignats could only be offered in payment at a sale of public lands. The mandats never obtained circulation as money, but fell at once into the hands of speculators. When first issued, they soon were only worth $\frac{1}{70}$th of their nominal value, and in the course of 1796 they were returned to the Government in payment of taxes and lands. In July, 1796, the whole system of paper money came to an end by the enactment of a law permitting business to be transacted in any circulating medium, and making mandats receivable in payment of taxes only *at their current value in trade.* Mr. G. de Puynode, in his able and interesting work, "De la Monnaie, du credit et de l'impot," says, "such are the terrible perturbations produced in communities by a forced circulation of paper money. An inevitable fatality urges the Governments that use it, toward its abuse ; for a forced circulation of paper money is always resorted to in moments of crisis, when the ordinary resources are insufficient. A first excess in the issue of paper money, rendered necessary by excessive expenditures, produces a depreciation in the value of the money received in payment of the taxes levied, and this depreciation obliges the Government to make further issues to augment its resources, so as to compensate the depreciation in the value of the taxes ; and so on, *ad infinitum*, until the value of the paper falls to zero, which is equivalent to general, or rather national bankruptcy."

*Progress of the emission of assignats, and of their depreciation.*

| | | | Discount. |
|---|---|---|---|
| The amount of the first emission of 1st April, 1790, was, . . | 400 | million frs. | |
| They had reached, by the end of 1790, . . . . . | 1,200 | " | 10 per cent. |
| The amount in Sept., 1792, was, | 2,700 | " | 37 " |
| " Sept., 1793, was, | 5,000 | " | 55 " |

After this, a forced loan was decreed, that redeemed 840 millions, which were burned ; but by the beginning of 1794, new issues had raised the amount to over 5,000 millions.

| | | | Discount. |
|---|---|---|---|
| The amount in June, 1794, was, | 6,636 | million frs. | |
| " March, 1795, was, | 8,000 | " | 78 per cent. |
| " Oct., 1795, was, | 19,000 | " | |

About this time, to obtain silver, 3,000 millions were issued, which produced but little over 100 millions in coin.

| | | Discount. |
|---|---|---|
| The amount at the end of 1795 was, . . . . . | 20,000 million frs., | 99 per cent. |
| And in Feb., 1796, . . . | 45,578 | " |

when they were entirely abandoned, and became utterly worthless.

The first issue of paper money in Russia was at the close of 1768, in the reign of Catherine II, when the Bank of Assignats was founded. The whole issue was limited to 400 millions of roubles. They were at first redeemed indifferently in silver or copper coin, but soon they were only redeemed in copper, which was overvalued by 50 per cent. From 1769 to 1787 the amount in circulation remained uniform at about 40 millions, and the agio in favor of silver varied from one to three per cent. in that interval, while there was an agio of from one to five per cent. in favor of the paper against copper. In 1774 they rose fully to par compared with silver. In 1787 a sudden addition was made of 60 millions, accompanied with a promise that no further quantity should be issued ; but a succession of wars with Turkey, Sweden, Poland, and Persia, and finally with France, caused the transgression of the promise, and further progressive issues were made till 1810, when they amounted, in the whole, to 577 millions ; and in 1817, to 836 millions. An increasing agio on silver was the consequence, till in October, 1816, the silver rouble was worth four in paper. During the progress of this depreciation of the paper, the customhouse duties, which were payable in silver money, could be paid in paper at an agio settled periodically upon a reference to the market rates. In October, 1816, the bank notes were declared by the Government to be receivable in payment of duties in the proportion of 4 to 1, thus officially acknowledging a depreciation of 75 per cent. On Jan. 1, 1821, the issues had been reduced to 640 millions, and the exchanges had improved so as to induce the Government to accept the paper rouble in payment of taxes at 3.60 for 1, and eventually at 3.50 for 1, at which last rate the conversion of bank assignats into bank notes payable on demand in silver roubles, was ordained by an imperial ukase, dated July 1, 1839.*

Our last illustration of government paper issues is that which occurred in the United States.

The old States, when colonies, to meet Indian and colonial war expenditures, issued paper money as far back as 1690, often at a considerable depreciation from their nominal value. Massachusetts alone issued from two to three millions of pounds lawful currency. In 1748 these issues of paper money were worth as follows :

| | | | | | |
|---|---|---|---|---|---|
| In New England, | £1100 | lawful | were | worth | £100 sterling.† |
| In New York, | 190 | " | " | " | " |
| In East Jersey, | 190 | " | " | " | " |
| In West Jersey, | 180 | " | " | " | " |
| In Pennsylvania, | 180 | " | " | " | " |
| In Maryland, | 200 | " | " | " | " |
| In Virginia, | 120 to 125 | " | " | " | " |
| In North Carolina, | 1000 | " | " | " | " |
| In South Carolina, | 700 | " | " | " | " |

* Tooke, History of Prices, vol. ii, p. 68—vol. iii, pp. 210, 215.

† The Funding System of the United States and Great Britain, by Jonathan Elliott, pp. 15, 16.

In the year 1749, the colony of Massachusetts had issued about £2,200,000 in bills of credit, as the government paper money was then called. The colony then obtained from Parliament a grant of £180,000 sterling in reimbursement of the expenses incurred by the colony in taking and securing Cape Breton from the French. The House of Representatives of Massachusetts passed an act in that year for establishing a stable currency of gold and silver. The act provided that the bills of credit outstanding should be redeemed at *eleven for one* with the sum granted by Parliament, which was to be shipped from England in Spanish milled dollars. This would leave about £220,000 in bills of credit outstanding, which were to be redeemed at the same rate by a tax on the year 1749. The act, after many weeks spent in debate, was rejected, but subsequently reconsidered, passed by the House and Council, and approved by the Governor. The measure proved perfectly successful. The apprehensions of a shock to trade proved groundless; the bills being dispersed through every part of the province, the silver took their place, a good currency was insensibly substituted in the room of a bad one, and every branch of business was carried on to greater advantage than ever.*

The following account of the issues of continental paper money during the war of Independence is taken from the writings of Thomas Jefferson, by H. A. Washington, vol. ix, pp. 248–259.

"On the commencement of the late Revolution, Congress had no money. The external commerce of the States being suppressed, the farmer could not sell his produce, and, of course, could not pay

* Gouge on Banking, p. 10.

a tax. Congress had no resource then but in paper money. Not being able to lay a tax for its redemption, they could only promise that taxes should be laid for that purpose, so as to redeem the bills by a certain day. They did not foresee the long continuance of the war, the almost total suppression of their exports, and other events, which rendered the performance of their engagement impossible. The paper money continued for a twelvemonth equal to gold and silver. But the quantities which they were obliged to emit for the purpose of the war, exceeded what had been the usual quantity of the circulating medium. It began, therefore, to become cheaper, or, as we expressed it, it depreciated, as gold and silver would have done, had they been thrown into circulation in equal quantities. But not having, like them, an intrinsic value, its depreciation was more rapid and greater than could ever have happened with them. In two years, it had fallen to two dollars of paper money for one of silver; in three years, to four for one; in nine months more, it fell to ten for one; and in the six months following, that is to say, by September, 1779, it had fallen to twenty for one.

"Congress, alarmed at the consequences which were to be apprehended should they lose this resource altogether, thought it necessary to make a vigorous effort to stop its further depreciation. They therefore determined, in the first place, that their emissions should not exceed two hundred millions of dollars, to which term they were then nearly arrived; and though they knew that twenty dollars of what they were then issuing would buy no more for their army than one silver dollar would buy, yet they thought it would be worth while to submit to the sacrifice of nineteen out of twenty dollars, if they could thereby stop further depreciation. They, therefore, published an address to their constituents, in which they renewed their original declarations that this paper money should be redeemed at dollar for dollar. They proved the ability of the States to do this, and that their liberty would be cheaply bought at that price. The declaration was ineffectual. No man received the money at a better rate; on the contrary, in six months more, that is, by March, 1780, it had fallen to forty for one. Congress then tried an experiment of a different kind. Considering their former offers to redeem this money at par as relinquished by the general refusal to take it, but in progressive depreciation, they required the whole to be brought in, declared it should be redeemed at its present value of forty for one, and that they would give to the holders new bills reduced in their denomination to the sum of gold or silver which was actually to be paid for them. This would reduce the nominal sum of the mass in circulation to the present worth of that mass, which was five millions; a sum not too great for the circulation of the States, and which, they therefore hoped, would not depreciate further, as they continued firm in their purpose of emitting no more. This effort was as unavailing as the former. Very little of the money was brought in. It continued to circulate and to depreciate till the end of 1780, when it had fallen to seventy-five for one, and the money circulated from the French army being by that time sensible in all the States north of the Potomac, the paper ceased its circulation altogether in those States. In Virginia and North Carolina it continued a year longer, within which time it fell to one thousand for one, and then expired, as it had done in the other States, without a single groan. Not a murmur was heard on this occasion, among the people; on the contrary, universal congratulations took place on their seeing this gigantic mass, whose dissolution had threatened convulsions which should shake their infant confederacy to its centre, quietly interred in its grave."

When the continental money was first issued, an expression of doubt as to its value involved suspicion of disaffection to the cause of the country. As the issues increased the price of goods necessarily rose; but this was attributed to combinations of the merchants to raise the price of their merchandise, and to sink the value of continental money. They were called tories, speculators, and many other hard names; their stores were forcibly broken open, and their goods sold at limited prices by committees of their neighbors.

Congress, as early as January 11th, 1776, resolved that "whoever should refuse to receive in payment continental bills, should be declared and treated as an enemy of his country, and be precluded from intercourse with its inhabitants," *i. e.* should be *outlawed.*

"This ruinous principle was continued in practice for five successive years, and appeared in all shapes and forms, *i. e.* in *tender acts; in limitations of prices: in awful and threatening declarations ; in penal laws,* with dreadful and ruinous punishments ; and in every other way that could be devised ; and all executed with a relentless severity by the highest authorities then in being, viz., by Congress, by assemblies and conventions of the States, and by committees of inspection (whose powers in those days were nearly sovereign), and even by military force ; and though men of all descriptions stood trembling before this monster of force, without daring to lift a hand against it during all this period, yet its unrestrained energy always proved ineffectual to its purposes, but in every case increased the evils it was designed to remedy, and destroyed the benefits it was intended to promote. Many thousand families of full and easy fortune were ruined by these fatal measures, without the least benefit to the country, or to the great and noble cause in which we were then engaged." *

The issues began 10th May, 1775, and ended in 1781. The depreciation began in about three years after the first issues.

| | | | | | |
|---|---|---|---|---|---|
| On March 1, 1778, | $1 in coin | was given | for | $1.75 | in paper money. |
| On Sept. 1, 1778, | " | " | " | 4.00 | " |
| On March 1, 1779, | " | " | " | 10.00 | " |
| On Sept. 1, 1779, | " | " | " | 18.00 | " |
| On March 18, 1780, | " | " | " | 40.00 | " |

* Pelatiah Webster, a merchant of Philadelphia, who published a series

A resolution was then passed by the old Congress, to fund them at $40 for $1, and interest to be paid on the new certificates. But the depreciation still went on.*

On Dec. 1, 1780, $1, in coin was given for $100 in paper money.
On May 1, 1781, " " " 200 to 500 "

They did not circulate as a currency after this ; but they passed at times at $1 for $1000 or more. The certificates bearing interest, issued for the paper money funded at $40 for $1, also rapidly depreciated, $8 being sold for $1 in coin, before 1791.

In 1791 a law was passed which *permitted* the continental paper money still outstanding to be funded at $100 for $1. The amount still outstanding in 1791 was estimated at from 78 to 80 millions of dollars.

| | New Emissions. | Old Emissions. |
|---|---|---|
| Alexander Hamilton in 1790 estimated the entire issues at.... | $2,070,485 | $357,476,541 |
| George on Banking, estimates the entire issue at.............. | 2,070,240 | 337,470,541 |
| Merchants' Magazine for January, 1843...................... | 2,071,085 | 387,476,337 |
| Amount as reported by the Treasury Department to the Senate, February 25, 1843.......... | | 242,100,176 |

of pamphlets on the subject, from 1776 to 1780, collected into a volume with notes in 1790. (Quoted by Gouge on Banking, pp. 11, 12.)

* " In the later stages of a depreciation, the rate at which it progresses is much more rapid than at the earlier stages. Naturally and inevitably this is so. Excessive quantity is one cause of depreciation, and growing distrust another. As soon as the latter is added to the former, the degradation is intensified; no one likes to hold that which is depreciating obviously and rapidly; every one passes it forward, and thus the downward motion is inevitably and constantly accelerated." (London Economist, 22d November, 1862.)

We find it impossible to decide which of these statements is correct.

Nearly all the government paper issues ever made have shared the same fate as those whose history we have sketched. The phases through which they all pass is remarkably similar. The issue of paper money is generally resorted to by governments, in moments of financial embarassments, as a resource to meet indispensable expenditures. This is contrary to the first principle of money, which is, that being an instrument made by the government *at the expense and for the convenience and advantage of the individuals who use it*, it should only be manufactured when demanded by the individuals. The principle which controls the issue of government paper money being false, like all other recourse to false principles, the issue cannot fail to be injurious to both government and people. No matter how despotic or popular the government issuing the paper money may be, the public soon lose confidence in it : if forced by legal enactments to accept it, they avoid holding it, and hoard the coin, in which they have confidence, and which, therefore, suddenly disappears from circulation. The anxiety to exchange paper money, in which the community has no confidence, for commodities and other property which have an intrinsic value, soon produces a rapid rise of prices, which is the true indication and measure of the depreciation of all paper money having a forced circulation. Every rise in prices, being in reality a fall in the value of the paper money, instead of inducing holders of commodities and property to realize, only increases their desire to retain them, whilst it increases the desire of the holders of paper money to exchange it for anything possessing intrinsic value. The inevitable result is a panic in regard to the paper money, and the very government that issued it is soon forced to refuse it in payment of taxes and loans, as it will no longer procure the supplies needed by the goverment and by its officers and employees.

## CHAPTER VII.

THE results of individual and corporate issues of paper money are in striking contrast with those of government.

Take for example the Scotch banks. These institutions have rendered incalculable services to the commerce and industry of Scotland. They have long been numerous in the midst of a small population, and are enterprising and active in a country of limited extent, with few manufacturing centres. The Scotch banks knew no law but *liberty* and *self-interest.* Until 1845 they were the freest banks that ever existed. Legislation limited neither their number, nor the number of their shareholders, nor their capital, nor the amount or nature of their issues, nor any other of their operations. From 1800 to 1814, owing to the scarcity of coin, they issued notes as low as 3 shillings. In 1826, out of a circulation of £3,309,052, £2,079,344 were *under* £5. In 1836 the circulation was £3,800,000, of which two thirds were under £5.

| | | | | | |
|---|---|---|---|---|---|
| There were | in Scotland | in 1825, 34 | banks having | 133 | branches. |
| " | " | 1850, 18 | " | 382 | " |
| " | " | 1859, | " | 583 | " |

All the shareholders are personally responsible for the debts of each bank, except those of the three incorporated banks, the Bank of Scotland, the Royal Bank of Scotland, and the British Linen Company, whose stockholders, by the acts of incorporation, are exempted from personal liability. There can be no doubt but that this personal liability tends to maintain a vigilant watch on the management of these institutions, besides which it offers a perfect and ample guarantee to the holders of the bank notes.

In 1841, the treasurer of the Bank of Scotland testified before a committee of the House of Commons, "that 7 millions in notes are found to be requisite to keep up an average circulation of 3 millions. It appears that the whole amount is out in circulation for a few days only at two seasons of the year." * Every note issued returned to the bank that issued it, within 10 or 11 days. This rapid return of the bank notes is fully explained by the conditions of a large portion of the advances made to the dealers, called cash credits. The dealer, to obtain one of these credits, must furnish two or more securities, who are jointly bound for the repayment of the advances of the bank. A credit is then opened, and the dealer may draw for the whole or part at any time; he may pay in, any day, whatever funds he receives, and only pays interest on the daily balance due by him to the bank.† It becomes thus the interest of the persons obtaining loans to pay in daily, on account, every trifling amount they may receive. How can over issues take place under such a system? How can and

* Tooke, History of Prices, vol. iii, p. 237.

† Encyclopædia Britannica, Money.

system be more beneficial to the dealers and to the community? How can any system economize currency to a greater extent? *

Although the circulation of the Scotch banks was not limited by law, it remained quite limited in extent, being regulated solely by the wants of the public. Coin is almost out of circulation in Scotland, being used only for change. McCulloch, in 1838, estimated the coin in circulation in Scotland at only £500,000. And yet the entire circulation of notes in Scotland does not exceed £3,500,000, whilst in England it has varied from 30 to 45 millions, being from twice to three times as great, in proportion to population, as in Scotland. † One of

* "Every bank, then, acts as a *centre of attraction* to draw out of circulation every £1 note which is not absolutely requisite to pay current expenses. Every Scotchman feels that he is losing money upon every note that he keeps idle in his pocket or in his house; every tradesman loses money for any sum he keeps idle in his till; the consequence of which is, that every one deposits with his banker all the cash he can spare, before the close of business hours, and so a large amount is withdrawn from visible circulation, which would go to swell the apparent amount of currency if it were not for this attractive power of the bank." (Macleod, Theory and Practice of Banking, vol. i, p. 410.)

"It is a remarkable circumstance that, while there has been a great extension of banking capital, and of banking accommodation, and of banking competition in Scotland since 1826, the amount of the aggregate circulation has considerably diminished. What a commentary upon the received doctrine of the power of banks to increase their issues of paper money as suits their interest or convenience; and that it is an effect of the competition of banks of issue to create a vast mass of worthless paper!" (Tooke, History of Prices, vol. iii, p. 237.)

† Mr. Anderson, manager of the Glasgow Union Banking Company, said, on his examination before a committee of the House of Commons in 1841, "We consider that the circulation does not require any regulation; our advances and loans we regulate, but not the circulation of our notes."

*Question* 2,369, by Sir James Graham: "Inasmuch as every payment into a bank, whether in the shape of a deposit, or to the credit of a current

the great regulators of the Scotch banks is the frequent exchanges of notes and liquidation of balances between them. Twice a week, the banks exchange and redeem their notes in Edinburgh, besides which, those of the west of Scotland exchange and redeem twice a week in Glasgow.

There have been but few failures of Scotch banks, and the losses of the public by them in 175 years, have been only £25,504, which is infinitely less than would have been the wear and tear of the coin required to effect the transactions performed by means of the banks.

account, bears interest day by day, and inasmuch as no commission is charged upon operations on an account, and inasmuch as a great proportion of the people receiving money in Scotland employ bankers, does it not follow that every payment made in local notes finds its way almost immediately within the space of twenty-four hours into the hands of some banker ?"

*Ans.* "I think it does."

*Q.* 2,370, by Mr. Grote : "Would not the consequence of that proposition be, if followed out, that there would be no notes whatever in the hands of the public, but that all the notes issued by each bank should be, in fact, in the hands of other banks ?"

*Ans.* "That is the effect. There are three millions of notes out, which is a very small amount; *people must have a certain amount of money in their pockets and boxes at home, and shopkeepers must keep a certain amount of money in their tills*, the daily receipts of their business; *and manufacturers must keep notes to pay people's wages, and so on ;* but that altogether proves but a small proportion compared to the circulation of England. Our three millions in Scotland amount to about £1 per head of the whole population; in England, although you have a gold circulation for everything below £5, your paper circulation amounts to £2 per head. I am taking about fifteen millions for the population, and thirty millions for the currency." (Tooke, History of Prices, vol. iii, pp. 241, 244, 245.)

The circulation of the Bank of England and of the English country banks in 1815 was £46,271,000.*

* Alison's History of Europe, vol. viii, p. 130. American edition.

Far from having produced financial crises, they have invariably prevented them. In 1824, when the English banks and bankers aided the wild speculations that prevailed, the Scotch Banks, on the contrary, contracted their loans. In 1836 and 1847, many English banks failed, but not a single Scotch bank ceased to grant their usual facilities to their dealers. Forgeries of the bank notes are unknown. The consequence is that the Scotch prefer their bank notes to gold, and make all their collections and payments through the banks, which leads to great economy in the use of both specie and bank notes.

In Scotland, each year the circulation becomes very much reduced in March—it increases in May—subsequently falls, though not as low as in March, and increases again to touch the highest point in November. Most of the payments in Scotland are made in May and November. These fluctuations occur each year, whether the banks increase or diminish in number; proving that they are produced by the wants of the community, and not by the wishes or action of the banks. Similar results in regard to the fluctuations of the currency occur in England and Ireland. In England the highest circulation is in April, and the lowest in August, also following the movements of commerce, industry, and agriculture. In Ireland the lowest circulation is in August and September, just before the harvests and the sales of cattle; and the highest in January, when the cattle and crops are sold.

"When the Government determined on suppressing the small note issues in England, the ministers said it was their intention to extend the measure in a short time to Scotland and Ireland. As soon as the ministerial intentions were known in Scotland, a great ferment was excited, and such an opposition was organized that the ministry were obliged to consent to appoint committees of both Houses on the subject. These committees sat during the spring of 1826, and investigated the whole subject of Scotch banking at great length, which had been very little understood in England before that time; and the result was so eminently favorable to the Scotch banking system, that the ministry abandoned their intention of attempting to alter it." *

In 1845, Sir Robert Peel obtained the enactment of a law regulating the Scotch banks, somewhat similar to the act of 1844 regulating the English banks. It prohibits all issues of notes under £1, and no bank created after May 1, 1845, can issue notes at all. The banks existing on the 1st May, 1845, may continue to issue notes, but are limited to the amount of their average circulation during the year ending on that day. Any notes issued beyond that amount must be represented by an equivalent amount of specie in their vaults, the idea being, as in England, to maintain a uniform amount of the entire circulation by means of a maximum amount of issues by each bank. Two or more banks may be consolidated into one, and the consolidated bank becomes entitled to issue the same amount of notes that could have been issued by the old banks before their consolidation. All the banks are obliged to forward to the directors of the stamp office, in London, weekly returns of their condition, which returns are published every four weeks in the

* Macleod, Theory and Practice of Banking, vol. i, pp. 262–263.

London *Gazette*. They are also obliged to send, once a year, a list of the names of all their stockholders.

All these limitations and prohibitions are as arbitrary as they are unreasonable.* Why prohibit notes under £1, when the notes of less amount had never been found injurious, but on the contrary advantageous? Why forever fix the relation of circulation and specie for a future unknown to all, particularly when all the writers on the subject, all the persons who testified before the committees appointed by Parliament, all the reports of those committees, bore the highest testimony in favor of the management of the Scotch banks and of the results of their operations? Why prohibit new banks of issue? The past proclaims the advantages of competition, and is not the future the echo of the past? Why exclude others from exercising rights similar to those possessed by the present banks? The enactment of laws regulating banking is undoubtedly a great error.† Should a commercial crisis now arise,

* "For more than a century no bank note was ever unpaid in Scotland, and it is inexplicable how Sir Robert Peel, with such a fact before his eyes, should have listened to empty theories about inflated circulation, excessive issues, and other sonorous phrases of like quality. Scotch notes have always been paid, because the Scotch have framed a sound system of securing the solvency of the issues; and had the Bank of England gone on issuing one-pound or ten-shilling notes since the Conquest, every one would have been paid in like manner. . . . In this, as in many other matters, the political logic of the Scotch nation has been admirable. They have followed out Adam Smith's doctrine to its just conclusion. They have suffered no arbitrary line to restrict the economy and convenience of a paper currency at the dictation of shallow dogmatism and caprice." (North British Review, November, 1861, What is Money?)

† "Governments have arrogated to themselves the task of regulating the currency, and the natural effect is, that nothing is less regular. At present, each day brings to London an abundant supply of fish, meat, vegetables, &c.,

the banks, their issues being limited, will no longer be able to grant their usual facilities to commerce. The community, pressed by their necessities, will be forced to withdraw a portion of their deposits. This will decrease their specie, and their circulation must therefore be still further diminished, and a financial crisis, a thing unknown in Scotland up to the present day,

and each day proves that the persons who furnish those supplies understand tolerably well what is required. Were government to *regulate* the markets as they do the currency, there would be a succession of over supplies, during which vast quantities of provisions would be spoiled, followed by a succession of scarcities, when double prices would be paid for the necessaries of life, precisely as is now the case with *money*. Whenever those who control the operations of government shall learn that the trade in money is like all other trades; that every man has *a right* to associate himself with his neighbors, and to trade with others on such terms as they may mutually deem most likely to be advantageous, whether of limited or unlimited liability, and that every man has *the same right* to furnish currency that he has to furnish hats, coats, or shoes; and whenever they shall abolish all restrictions thereupon, there may and will exist a good, sound, safe, and cheap currency, but not till then." (H. C. Carey, The Credit System, p. 122.)

"Various propositions have been made in regard to that of both England and the United States, by persons who believe that more steadiness would be obtained by having a single body or institution authorized to issue paper to be used therefor, and by others for preventing the circulation of notes under ten and twenty dollars, or pounds, &c. Experience, however, teaches that when governments undertake to regulate trade or commerce, to furnish roads or education, there is at one time, or in one place, an over supply, and at another, a deficiency. Such would be the case in regard to currency. Experience also teaches us that when the people undertake to supply themselves, and they are not restrained in their actions, the supply is well regulated. In no part of the world is the power of supplying currency so much divided, in none are silver and gold to so great a degree dispensed with, and in no country of the world is there one combining so many of the requisites of a perfect currency, as are to be found in that of Massachusetts and Rhode Island." (Id., ib., pp. 122, 123.)

will aggravate the commercial crisis.* Mr. Hume, in a debate in 1848, said, "with respect to the act of 1845 relating to Scotland, he ventured to say that there never was a more uncalled-for piece of legislation in the world. Not one single soul in Scotland was found to support it, and all the Scotch witnesses who were examined before the committee, spoke of its bad effects." †

Mr. G. du Puynode, from whose able work, "De la Monnaie, du credit, et de l'impot," we have compiled many of the preceding remarks on the Scotch banks, closes by saying, "No banks in the world have been so wisely, so prudently managed as the Scotch banks, and none have been so free from legislative control. It must be, therefore, that there are other and far preferable guarantees for the proper administration of banks, than those resorted to by legislators. Is it not truly a strange idea to ignore intelligence and morality (he should have added self-interest) as sources of capacity and stability? What admirable foresight to regulate everything, to order everything, in the midst of a present which we scarcely understand, in contradiction of a past admired by all, and in the face of a future entirely unknown! Without liberty and without competition there can be no true progress and no efficacious guarantees." ‡

Whenever the use of bank notes is controverted, it is usual to cite the United States as an example of

* G. du Puynode, De la Monnaie, du credit, et de l'impot, vol. i, pp. 270, 271, edition, 1853.

† Tooke, History of Prices, vol. v, p. 494.

‡ Vol. i, pp. 274, 275.

its pernicious effects. What is never done, however, is to furnish proofs to sustain that conclusion. Let us examine some facts in regard to the banks of the United States, during the period from 1811 to 1836. Mr. H. C. Carey says:* "The period from 1811 to 1836 embraces times of embargo, non-intercourse, war, suspension of specie payments, resumption thereof, change from a state of universal war to one of universal peace—that period, in short, which has, throughout the world, been attended by the most remarkable changes in the fortunes and prospects of individuals and of nations, which was most likely to exhibit extraordinary losses by individuals, and consequently by banks." This is by far the most trying period in the history of the American banks, and the results are, therefore, less favorable to them than would be shown by any other lengthened period that can be taken. The crisis of 1837–1839 entailed severe losses by bank failures in the Western and Southern States; but in the Eastern and Middle States, with the exception of the Bank of the United States of Philadelphia, they were quite moderate; and the greater part of the loss, everywhere, fell on the stockholders and not on the public. If banks and paper money were, as is so frequently asserted, injurious to the community, could they have increased so greatly in the United States, in spite of all the adverse circumstances that have occurred to try them? †

* The Credit System, p. 25.

† "The adoption of the same measures by which it has been attempted in the United States to drive bank notes out of circulation, would have ruined the banks of England and of France. Nothing could have prevented the ruin of those of the United States but the general confidence of man in his fellow man." (Id., ib., p. 37, note.)

There existed in the United States:

| | | | |
|---|---|---|---|
| In 1811, | 88 | banks with an aggregate capital of | $42,609,101 |
| 1816, | 246 | " " " " | 89,822,297 |
| 1820, | 307 | " " " " | 101,714,551 |
| 1830, | 328 | " " " " | 110,186,608 |
| 1838, | 677 | " " " " | 378,000,000 |

The average number of banks in the six New England States, Connecticut, Rhode Island, Massachusetts, New Hampshire, Vermont, and Maine, from 1811 to 1830, was 97, with a capital of about $22,000,000. In 1830 there were 172 banks, with a capital of $35,226,000. In twenty-five years the number of bank failures in that district was 16, with a capital of about $2,000,000. The total loss sustained by the community by these failures cannot have much exceeded $500,000, say an annual average of $20,000, or $\frac{1}{11}$th of one per cent. on the aggregate capital of all the banks, and probably about $\frac{1}{500}$th of one per cent. on the amount of the operations facilitated by those institutions. If this estimate be correct, the loss attending the transactions with the banks of New England, during more than a quarter of a century, has been, on an average, one dollar in $50,000. If we exclude Connecticut, in which one failure was attended with great frauds and resulted in great losses, the loss does not exceed five dollars per million.

Exactly as in Scotland, the circulation of bank

"The Americans have the utmost faith in paper money. It is not a blind confidence; for if we have had our *assignats*, they have had their continental money; and it would not be necessary to retrace their history far to find the banks failing 'en masse.' It is a confidence founded upon reason—a courage the result of reflection." (M. Chevalier's United States, vol. ii, p. 247.)

notes in New England is very moderate, in consequence of the activity of the circulation and the general resort by the inhabitants to their banks for all their payments and collections. The circulation in 1830, notwithstanding, or we should rather say, in consequence of the great number of the banks, only amounted to $13,992,-000. With an aggregate capital of $35,226,000, their discounts only amounted to $46,759,000, and they held in specie $2,607,000. Their circulation and their advances to their dealers remain therefore quite limited in proportion to their means.* Moreover, again exactly as in Scotland, specie is hardly ever seen in this portion of the United States; the bank notes suffice for nearly every transaction. In the midst of extensive commercial transactions, in a district where an excessively laborious trading population are incessantly operating, the entire circulation is only $7½ per capita, of which $2 is specie; and yet this amount is found to be ample. In France, where the amount of transactions is proportionally much smaller, it is estimated that the metallic circulation alone is about 100 francs ($20) per capita. What expense, what labor and lack of confidence do the latter figures reveal; and on the contrary, what confidence, ease, and economy do the former indicate! We

| | Bank Capital. | Total Currency. | Specie in Banks. | Am't of Loans. |
|---|---|---|---|---|
| * New England, 1830, | $35,226,000 | $13,992,000 | $2,607,000 | $46,759,000 |
| Bank of England, | £15,000,000 | £30,000,000 | £8,000,000 | £37,000,000 |

The currency furnished by the Bank of England is twice the amount of its capital, whereas that furnished by the banks of New England is only one third of their capital. In England it requires an unemployed capital invested in gold, in bank, sixteen times as great as that of New England, in addition to a larger quantity in circulation, while the amount of its business is but little more than four times as great." (H. C. Carey, The Credit System, p. 71.)

have before us, apparently two entirely different societies, two different civilizations.*

In the State of New York, during the period from 1811 to 1830, the loss of the community, by the failure of banks, apart from that of the stockholders, cannot have exceeded $5 per million of the circulation, and probably not $1 per million of the transactions they have aided.

In 1830 the entire capital of the banks of the States of New York, New Jersey, and Pennsylvania amounted to $9 per inhabitant, being less than one half of the amount at that period in New England, which was $19½ per inhabitant. On the other hand, their discounts amounted to double the amount of their capital, whereas in New England, the discounts were not quite one third more than the amount of the capital of the banks. In Pennsylvania, where the banks were not allowed to issue notes under $5, and where consequently specie forms a considerable portion of the circulation, the bank notes in circulation are greater in proportion to the capital of the banks than in Massachusetts. We have evidence here that the freer and

| | | | Days. |
|---|---|---|---|
| * "The currency of France is equal to the production of the nation for | | | 144 |
| That of England is equal to | " | " | 110 |
| That of the United States is equal to | " | " | 23 |
| That of New England is equal to | " | " | 21 |

(H. C. Carey, The Credit System, p. 73.)

"New England maintains a currency at less cost than any other part of the world." (Id., ib., p. 108.)

"The *increase* of confidence manifested by the substitution of bank notes, checks, and drafts, for gold and silver, tends, therefore, to *diminish the proportion of capital* required for the performance of exchanges, and to *increase the productiveness of labor*." (Id., ib., p. 130.)

the more numerous are the banks, the greater is the capital that guarantees their operations.

Taking the aggregate of the banks of New England, New York, New Jersey, and Pennsylvania, during the period from 1811 to 1830, the entire losses of the public by bank failures cannot exceed $\frac{1}{400}$th of one per cent. on the transactions made by means of those institutions. During the last fifteen years of the period they do not exceed $5 per million, and probably do not even reach $1 per million.

The total number of bank failures in the United States from 1811 to 1836 were 167, of which 130 south and west of the State of New York. The average number of banks in operation during the same period was 242. The average number of failures has been therefore 2¾ per cent., which is only a trifle over the average failures among the private banks of England during the period from 1821 to 1826; a period which includes, it is true, the great commercial crisis of 1825, but which was marked by no other extraordinary event, such as a transition from war to peace, or from peace to war, that might cause universal disasters of this nature. From the first institution of banks in the United States, to the year 1837, the bank failures have been about ¼ less than those that occurred in England during the three years, 1814, 1815, and 1816; and the losses sustained by the public are probably still less relatively to the amount of the transactions effected by means of the banks in the two countries. In the presence of such facts, what justice is there in the accusations so frequently made of unskilfulness and improvidence in the management of the American banks?

In the United States the total circulation does not exceed ordinarily $9 per inhabitant, of which one quarter, at most, is specie; whilst in England it amounts to $28 per inhabitant, of which one third is specie. In France the difference is probably twice as great, and it is well known that the greater part of the circulation in that country is specie.* The reason of the larger circulation in France than in England and in the United States, is self-evident. Every community must have, at any moment, the amount of currency necessary to transact the exchanges then taking place. Where coin alone is used, when commerce and industry require an increase of the circulation, it can only be obtained from private hoards of specie made in moments when the specie is in excess of the demand, and the circulation is therefore contracting; or when specie is imported in excess of the immediate wants of the community.† The community is thus forced to keep on hand at all times an amount of coin equal to the maximum amount used, no matter for how short a period a portion of it may be required; and to obtain this coin the country must part with an equivalent amount of real, useful capital, of

* This synopsis of the American banks is mostly taken from "De la Monnaie, du credit, et de l'impot," by G. de Puynode, who derived the facts from "The Credit System," by H. C. Carey, of Philadelphia.

† "The hoards absorb the superfluous produce of the mines when it is overflowing, and disgorge it again when it is wanted for use; so that the fluctuations of supply and demand do not affect at all that portion of the coin which circulates, and which alone operates on prices, but only that portion which is hoarded. (Fullarton on the Regulation of Currencies, p. 71.)

"Upon the action of the hoards depends the whole economy of the international payments between specie-circulating communities; while any operation of the money collected in hoards upon prices must, even according to the currency hypothesis, be wholly impossible." (Id., ib., p. 132.)

commodities that contribute to the well being and progress of all. But where the exchanges are effected with bank notes, the issues are increased at those moments when the exchanges or payments are large, and they contract, by the return of the superfluous notes to the banks that issued them, as soon as the exchanges or payments diminish.* This keeps down the circulation, at all times, to the lowest possible amount required to effect the exchanges or payments taking place. Thus the banks in Scotland require seven millions of notes to attain an average circulation of only three millions. Can any system of currency be more perfect or more advantageous than this? It facilitates the exchanges of commodities even better than coin, except with foreign nations; when properly managed, it expands and contracts in exact accordance with the transactions of commerce and industry, while it does not, like coin, absorb a large portion of the capital of the community.

* "Where the currency is purely metallic, the additional circulation required for these occasions would be drawn from the private hoards; while, wherever the credit system prevails, the circulation is supplied by the banks." (Fullarton on the Regulation of Currencies, p. 103.)

# CHAPTER VIII.

HAVING sketched the striking contrasts between the results of the issues of government paper money, and of bank notes, let us attempt to deduce from them the natural laws that govern paper money.

Money, as used in modern civilized communities, is a useful instrument that facilitates the exchanges of commodities and services.* Anything can perform the functions of money, as long as the community has full confidence that it will, at all times, command the com-

* "The use of the currency is to facilitate the transference of debts OR SERVICES DUE from one person to another, and whatever means be adopted for this purpose, whether it be gold, silver, or paper, is a currency; . . . therefore, . . . *currency and transferable debt are convertible terms:* whatever represents transferable debt of any description is currency; and whatever material the currency may consist of, it represents transferable debt and nothing else." (Macleod, Theory and Practice of Banking, vol. i, p. 25.)

"If we buy a sack of wheat, we do so because it possesses certain known qualities which are decidedly useful to us; we therefore buy a sack of wheat for its own sake. But we do not seek to obtain coin for its own sake; it is not capable of being put to any useful purpose directly, but we strive to obtain coin for the sake of the power it confers on its possessor of obtaining anything else that may suit his fancy; for the sake of the power it has of commanding the services of others; and if anything else besides coin possessed the same power, it would be equally desirable with the coin itself." (Id., ib., vol. i, p. 389.)

modities and services that may be required; but any money will soon be discarded when it ceases to command the commodities and services desired. It is the universal confidence in gold and silver as money, that has thus far made these metals the most reliable instruments of exchanges, as well as the most certain measures of value. But were paper money to inspire the same confidence and be as universally accepted as gold and silver, it would perform all the functions of money even better than those metals, as it is lighter, more easily transported and counted, far more economical, and more easily increased and decreased in amount, in accordance with the wants of the community.* It is a mistake to suppose that a thing, to perform successfully the functions of money, must possess intrinsic value.

* "Whether money has any value *in itself*, whether, as substances or as materials, it is an object of desire or not, this for the purposes of society, which is *dispatch of business*, is as indifferent as the nature of the yard-stick. If it *measures values* and effects exchanges, if it *marks a price*, and if it *passes*, it is good money. The best money is that which performs these functions with the greatest accuracy, with the greatest economy, and with the greatest convenience."

"The superiority of bank money over coin for convenience, economy, safety and dispatch of business . . . is so great, that were it not for other considerations, the use of coin, in every country, ought to be set aside entirely." (Bankers' Magazine, New York, August, 1846.)

"There is clearly no difference in principle between a metallic and a paper currency, only one depends upon *a wider basis of credit* than the other. . . . If it were possible to have a paper currency, based upon the same credit, and which should be as generally received as the metallic currency, it would be a preferable form." (Macleod, Theory and Practice of Banking, vol. i, p. 30.)

"Every man desires money because he can therewith procure whatever else he desires. If paper can procure for him the object of his desire as readily as gold and silver, paper is as desirable to him as gold and silver." (Gouge on Banking, p. 13.)

Money, at present, whatever may have been the case in olden times, measures the relative value of things, and is beneficially used as a medium of effecting exchanges, not because of its intrinsic value, but simply because it is universally accepted in exchange for all things. Intrinsic value was necessary in the infancy of civilization, when the slight development given to the division of labor, and consequently to the exchanges of commodities and services, rendered it important that anything received in exchange should possess intrinsic, useful qualities, since it was principally with a view to consumption that it was accepted.* But at the present day, the infinite and constantly increasing division of labor has given such immense importance to the exchanges of all things, that money, as a mere instrument for facilitating these exchanges, is infinitely more useful to humanity than any commodity whatever, as the possession of current money places all things at our com-

* "Intrinsic value was indispensably necessary at first to give circulation, because barter was kept in mind; but in process of time, when money became in use, that is entirely lost sight of. It is taken as money, without reference to its intrinsic value. If gold and silver were to lose all value independent of their character as money, would they be stript of their character as money?" (Rees, Encyclopædia, Money.)

"The simplest and most perfect form of a currency is that which represents nothing but transferable debt, and of which the material is of no intrinsic value, such as paper. It is only when states have reached a high degree of civilization that they adopt this perfect form; before they attain that, the material of it entirely consists of something which has an intrinsic value, such as gold or silver. But this intrinsic value is a secondary circumstance, and not the one which gives it its characteristic as a currency. *It is its general reception as the visible symbol of transferable power*, which is also called negotiability, which is the essence of a currency, and distinguishes a coin from a medal." (Macleod, Theory and Practice of Banking, vol. i, p. 45.)

mand. But, to this end, the thing used as money must be universally received, at all times, in exchange for commodities and services; and this cannot be unless the commodities themselves, and the persons able to render the services desired, exist. In a desert island, or in a besieged town, money, at times, is nearly useless, because the things desired do not exist there. It is, therefore, evident that paper money, to perform successfully the functions of money, should never be issued except against a pledge, direct or indirect, of a greater value of useful commodities, needed by the community, applicable to the redemption of the bank notes issued. Such a rule, strictly adhered to, would make paper money a perfect instrument of exchanges, because the redemption of bank notes in commodities and services is preferable to their redemption in coin; for commodities and services are useful *per se*, whilst the only use of coin is as means of obtaining those very commodities and services.* The redemption of bank notes in commodities and services through the clearing

* "Currency, then, being merely a symbol of the power of commanding services, it is clearly not the possession of the currency, but the services it can command, that constitute the wealth of the possessor, and it is only as it represents these services that currency can be considered as wealth. Currency in its stagnant state is not wealth; sovereigns or bank notes lying idle in a box are of no use to their owner; they are neither meat, nor drink, nor clothing, nor fuel, nor shelter, nor anything else that is useful; but they are the proof that their owner has the right to get all these things when he requires them. . . . It is the right and power of the possessor of currency to command the services of the community, that constitute his wealth, and not the mere evidence of it contained in the currency he holds; and the less costly the material which contains this evidence, provided it be effectual for its purpose, the better it is." (Macleod, Theory and Practice of Banking, vol. i, pp. 45, 46.)

house of the industry of the world, from which every one withdraws precisely the things he desires in exchange for the bank notes he holds, is the beau ideal of money under the present system of the infinite division of labor. Under such a system, paper money becomes a mere certificate of services rendered, for which the holder has not been remunerated.* Each holder, by transferring the certificate, transfers his claim to any parties that render him an equivalent service. The redemption of money in commodities and services (by this phrase, wherever used, is meant the general acceptance of money in exchange for commodities and services) is the main requisite to the proper fulfilment of the functions of money, and is just as indispensable to the precious metals as to paper money. Bank notes are made redeemable in coin, only because coin is, as yet, more universally accepted in exchange for commodities and services than bank notes.† The precious

* "Currency is nothing more than the evidence of services having been rendered, for which an equivalent has not been received, but can at any time be demanded." (Macleod, Theory and Practice of Banking, vol. i, p. 24.)

"When the laborer has received his wages in money, he has not received an equivalent for his services, but only something which will enable him to get what he requires or chooses. The money, therefore, that he possesses, is not *the equivalent*, but it is the symbol or proof that he has rendered services for which he has *not yet received an equivalent*." (Id., ib., vol. ii, p. xliv.)

† "Instead of representing services or commodities directly, it is almost invariably usual to make the paper currency of a country represent a certain portion of the metallic currency, which is the generally received representative of all services and commodities." (Id., ib., vol. i, p. 30.)

"Paper money should be represented by commodities. To insure this, it is made convertible into the best known commodities, gold and silver." (Encyclopædia Britannica, Money.)

metals circulate everywhere; bank notes only within a more or less restricted circle around the place of their issue. The object in presenting bank notes for redemption in coin, as long as they are in good credit, is invariably to procure with the coin commodities in localities where the bank notes are not accepted because unknown.

Government paper money cannot, successfully, for any length of time, perform the functions of money, because it is invariably issued as a financial resource, in moments of emergency, generally when war is ruthlessly destroying both life and property. Government paper money, instead of representing existing results of labor, ready to redeem the paper money on demand of the holders, only represents property and lives consumed or destroyed, and labor unproductively employed. How can such paper issues long perform the functions of money, when even metallic money cannot perform them unless constantly redeemed with useful results of labor and with useful services? Money cannot be redeemed with useful results of labor, unless these have been produced, economized, and thus exist for those who desire them in exchange for money. It will be said that the entire property of a nation is pledged for the redemption of the paper money issued by its government. But all this property is in the hands of individuals, who rely upon it for their own well being and enjoyment, as well as to meet their own liabilities; and they never consent that any large portion of the results of their labor shall be taken from them for the use of the government or its creditors. Even the small portion they are willing to contribute for that purpose, can only be reached by levying taxes; and the right of taxation to meet state indebtedness is rarely exercised by governments when it becomes unpopular, because burdensome. History bears abundant witness to this incontrovertible fact.

The result of all past experience in regard to paper money, is conclusive as to the superiority of individual and corporation issues over government issues ; and the more we analyze the question, the clearer this becomes. Government paper money does not possess a single element of the indispensable functions of money, except that of being received in payment of taxes ; and that is almost invariably withdrawn from it as soon as it depreciates in value to any extent, because governments can no more use a depreciated currency than individuals. Government paper money cannot inspire general confidence, because it is affected by every unfavorable political event, by wars and revolutions. These events have much less effect on bank notes issued against commodities, because commodities are always necessary or useful to the community, and, in time of war, generally rise in value from the diversion of labor from industry to war. Government paper money cannot long inspire general confidence, because the very issue of a compulsory government paper money, is a conclusive proof of impoverished and embarrassed finances, and every subsequent issue is an evidence of increasing embarrassment and poverty. Government paper money also lacks that important element of confidence which bank notes offer : the power of the holders to enforce payment by legal measures. An individual cannot enforce by legal means the most sacred claim against a government. Its payment depends entirely on the will of those who administer the government. This greatly contributes to the rapid depreciation of government paper money when confidence in it is once shaken. Laws making government paper money a legal tender cannot arrest its depreciation when confidence in it becomes impaired. Such a law can, momentarily, rob the creditor classes for the benefit of their debtors ; but no government, however despotic, has yet succeeded in compelling producers to produce, and dealers to sell, commodities at a loss ; and every attempt to do this, only disorganizes industry to the great injury of all. If the injury caused by a forced circulation of government paper money could be limited to the loss through the depreciation it experiences, it might yet be submitted to. But unfortunately the moment the depreciation becomes considerable, the paper money drives out of circulation all metallic money, which is then hoarded, and the paper money itself ceases to perform the proper functions of money ; the community are thus deprived of the indispensable instrument, money, by which all exchanges are effected, and the final consequence invariably is, the cessation or diminution of production, for no one will produce commodities when they cannot be readily exchanged for whatever he desires. If governments, when they think it necessary to issue paper, would only allow it to pass at whatever value the public might put upon it, it would be infinitely better for all, as the exchanges between individuals and with foreign nations would then go on uninterrupted, and production would rather be stimulated than impeded by the burdens entailed upon the community to meet the financial necessities of the government.*

* "If paper money or bank notes cannot be maintained on a par with

The moment that the depreciation of government paper money becomes considerable, this becomes a powerful, almost an irresistible argument in the hands of demagogues, in favor of its repudiation. The poorer classes are then arrayed against the rich, who are accused, as if it were a crime, of having purchased the paper money at a heavy discount, and, therefore, not entitled to its reimbursement. Every one then seems to forget that had not those who possessed capital purchased the paper money when it was offered at a discount, it would much sooner have fallen to zero.

Another grave objection to government paper money is that the amount and time of the issues is not, cannot be, regulated by the wants of the community, but solely by the necessities of the government.* A currency

gold, the next best thing is to allow all persons to receive the notes at whatever value they choose to put upon them. . . . If this be allowed, no very great inconvenience will take place in the internal trade of the country." (Macleod, Theory and Practice of Banking, vol. i, p. 336.)

* "When a government issues paper money, inconvertible and compulsorily current, it is usually in payment for

1. The personal expenditures of the sovereign or the governing power.
2. Public works or buildings.
3. Salaries of civil servants.
4. Maintenance of military and naval establishments.

It is quite clear that paper created and so paid away by the government, not being returnable to the issuer, will constitute a fresh source of demand (for commodities and services), and must be forced into and permeate all the channels of circulation. Accordingly, every fresh issue beyond the point at which former issues had settled in a certain rise of prices and of wages, and a fall (rise) of the exchanges, is soon followed by a further rise of commodities and wages and a fall (rise)† of the exchanges; the deprecia-

† What is designated in the United States a rise of exchanges, is, in England, called a fall of the exchanges, because a lesser amount of foreign coin is obtained in exchange for a pound sterling, and *vice versa*. The English expression is certainly very incorrect, and would mislead any one but an expert in banking.

should be elastic, should contract and expand in accordance with the volume of the exchanges it facilitates. This elasticy of the currency is of vast importance to the community, and is one of the great advantages paper money offers over coin, for *it is not by maintaining a uniform amount of currency in circulation that its value can be maintained uniform, but by maintaining a constant uniform relation between the amount of the currency and the amount of the exchanges it facilitates.**

In one word, government paper money offers none of the guarantees and attributes of a successful me-

tion being in the ratio of the forcibly increased amount of the issues.' (Tooke, History of Prices, vol. i, pp. 176, 177.)

* "The supply of the circulating medium in every country ought to be commensurate in quantity to the number and value of the exchanges which it has to perform. And as the number and value of such exchanges are liable to vary with every variation in the state of industry, as well as with the progress of population, it is obvious that the monetary system would be a very defective one, if the supply of the circulating medium did not vary in corresponding proportions." (Fullarton on the Regulation of Currencies, pp. 100, 101.)

"If any legislative interference with the currency at all be desirable, its aim should be to maintain its uniformity in value as far as possible. Now, uniformity in value does not mean uniformity in quantity, but uniformity in the amount of services it can command, and consequently it should increase or diminish in exact proportion to the amount of operations it represented. Thus in Scotland it was observed, that at certain periods of the year, the quantities of currency in circulation were subject to certain regular and well defined fluctuations, because at certain periods of the year a greater amount of operations took place than at others, and the Scotch banks were in the habit of increasing their issues in proportion to their operations, and it was this very fluctuation in quantity that prevented the uniformity in value, because the quantity of the currency in circulation always rose and fell in unison with the amount of operations; consequently the same amount of currency represented the same amount of service. If the currency had been limited in quantity, it would have caused the most violent fluctuations in value." (Macleod, Theory and Practice of Banking, vol. i, pp. 208, 209.)

dium of exchanges, and its issue should never be permitted by any people that have a voice in their government, and any regard for their own interest and well being.*

* "There is not, I believe, a single example on record, of the power of creating money out of cheap materials having been exercised by a sovereign state for any length of time, or through any season of public difficulty, without having been abused. So long as the whole supplies of the year are raised by means of taxes and loans, no great mischief can befall; for the paper which the state issues in its payments, will in that case all flow back again regularly, in the shape of loans and taxes, and there will be no surplus left to accumulate in the hands of the public. But say that the nation is once embarked in a destructive and expensive war, with little prospect of bringing it soon to a termination, that the revenues are failing, the government at its wit's end to discover some new tax that will supply the deficiency, and the impatience of such exactions on the part of the people already at its height,—the temptation to substitute issues for taxation, to relieve the wants of the treasury, by intercepting, through the depreciation of the currency, a portion of every payment in its transit from the pocket of the debtor to that of his creditor, becomes too strong to be resisted, and the iniquity is, probably, perpetrated with the general acquiescence of a community, who are scarcely aware of its tendency. The career of debasement once entered upon, it has no pause, till there is scarcely any value left to be destroyed. And if, in this country, the portentous experiment of the suspension of cash payments was not followed by the same disastrous consequences which attended the issues of the Mississippi notes, and the assignats in France, and of the several paper currencies put forth by the principal states of northern Europe, it was because the inconvertible notes were disbursed, not in payments of a government, but in the loans of a bank." (Fullarton on the Regulation of Currencies, p. 24.)

"It is not so much by convertibility into gold, as by the regularity of the reflux, that any redundance of the bank-note issues is rendered impossible; and it was by the preservation of the reflux, throughout all the perils and temptations of the period of the restriction, that the monetary system of these kingdoms was saved from the utter wreck and degradation which overwhelmed every paper-issuing state on the Continent, and which, in all human probability, must have been likewise our fate had the currency been issued by a government board instead of the Bank of England. That will be an evil day for England, when the supreme executive authority of this

As money must be constantly redeemed with commodities and services, paper money, to perform successfully the functions of money, should always represent useful commodities, or other results of labor, actually existing in the hands of persons willing to accept the paper money in exchange for them. Paper money, issued by an individual possessing commodities useful to the community, of greater value than the amount of paper money issued, can be as readily, and, *to the community, more advantageously* redeemed, by the sale of the commodities, than by gold and silver, because the purchasers of the commodities must, in exchange, either return the paper money issued, or something that will be readily accepted by the holders of the paper money. But to inspire full confidence in paper money issued against the pledge of commodities and other useful results of labor, it is further necessary to have entire confidence in the probity of the parties holding the commodities, so as to insure the conviction that they are of greater value than the paper money issued against them, and, also, that their proceeds, when sold, will be applied to the redemption of the paper money, and to nothing else. It is to meet this requirement that banks intervene beneficially. Banks with large capitals, subscribed by individuals, undertake the emission of bank notes, which they advance to the producers or holders of the commodities. The capital of the banks is an ample security for any deficiency in the value of the commodities against which the bank notes are loaned

country shall take the administration of a credit circulation into its own hands. I trust never to see it." (Fullarton on the Regulation of Currencies, pp. 67, 68.)

or issued, as well as for any misapplication of the proceeds of the commodities when sold. The self-interest of the stockholders and officers of the banks is a sufficient guarantee that the advances of bank notes will only be made to persons of known probity, possessed of ample property to insure the redemption of the bank notes advanced to them. But should the banks make improper advances, the consequences will fall on the stockholders, and not on the holders of its notes. The persons to whom the banks make advances of bank notes are merchants or manufacturers, who constantly watch, with the vigilance of self-interest, all the wants of the community, so as to produce, or purchase, the commodities most needed, and therefore most sought for, the proceeds of which will not only reimburse the advances of the banks, and that portion of their own capital invested in the commodities, but also leave them a remuneration for their labor and intelligence. This machinery has been found to work beneficially for all the parties in interest, the banks, the commercial and industrial classes, and the public, as is fully proved by the results of the operations of the banks of Scotland and of the United States.

It is constantly asserted that banks transform debts into money; that the same property, when sold on credit three times, becomes the basis of three different issues of bank notes or bank credits; thus transforming one amount of property into three times the same amount of purchasing power.* The following analysis

* "The same lot of goods might be sold to a dozen persons, and each might give a note, and each of these twelve notes might be discounted at

of commercial operations shows clearly that this theory is without foundation, being based on supposed facts that never occur; on an entire ignorance of the true philosophy of commerce and industry.

A is a capitalist that holds commodities which he has either produced or purchased with his capital. He sells to B, of these commodities, to the extent of $5,000, payable in a note at six months from date. This note thus represents the commodities in the hands of B, drawer of the note. A, desiring to purchase other commodities for cash, or to pay for commodities previously purchased on credit, has this note discounted by a bank, the proceeds of which he receives in bank notes, or in a bank credit, with which he pays for the new commodities purchased by him. There now exists an issue of bank notes or bank credits, based on, and represented by, twice the amount of commodities; those in the hands of B, purchased with the note given by

bank. The inducement then would be to buy and sell goods that notes might be discounted at bank." (Gouge on Banking, p. 19.)

"Goods or commodities pass through the following hands: First, the foreign importer or manufacturer; second, the wholesale dealer; third, the retail dealer; fourth, the consumer. It is clear that in their passage from the manufacturer to the consumer, they will give rise to at least two bills of exchange—not unfrequently to three. Now it is easy to suppose that the manufacturer, the wholesale dealer, and the retail dealer, may all be customers of the same bank, and if they all have their bills discounted by the bank, it may unknowingly advance money upon each of them, and so will advance on *bona fide* bills just three times the value of the property represented by them." (Macleod, Theory and Practice of Banking, vol. i, pp. 217–220.)

"In the most legitimate course of business there will generally be two bills afloat representing any given property, so that in the ordinary way there will be at least twice as many bills afloat as there is property to represent them." (Id., ib., vol. i, pp. 219, 220.)

him to A, and those in the hands of A, purchased with the bank notes or bank credits obtained by him in exchange for B's note, discounted by the bank. If B sells the commodities purchased of A to C, also on six months credit, and has C's note discounted at bank, so as to purchase new commodities for cash, or to pay for others previously purchased on credit, the position of things then becomes as follows:

1st. The bank holds B's note, represented by the commodities purchased by B with the bank notes issued to him in exchange for C's note, the proceeds of which commodities will pay B's note.

2d. The bank holds C's note, represented by the commodities purchased by him of B with this note, the proceeds of which commodities will pay C's note.

3d. A holds the commodities purchased by him with the bank notes issued to him in exchange for B's note, which commodities represent A's original capital, and are an additional guarantee for the payment of B's note, which A has indorsed when discounted by the bank.

We thus have here *three* parcels of commodities, each worth $5,000, against *two* issues of bank notes or bank credits of each $5,000, and not, as supposed by the theory, two issues of bank notes against one and the same property. Increase the number of sales of the same property *ad infinitum*, and it will always be found that for each new issue of bank notes appears a similar amount of new commodities, because commerce and industry only seek loans as means of purchasing or producing useful commodities; and thus there is a constant, uniform relation maintained between the issues of properly managed banks and existing commodities. Commodities consumed can never become the proper basis of an issue of bank notes. If each party that purchased and sold the same commodities on credit were to spend for their own personal enjoyment the bank notes received for the notes discounted, there would be several issues of bank notes entirely based on one and the same parcel of commodities ; but pay day would soon come—the drawers of the notes, having consumed their proceeds, would be unable to pay them, and the bank that had discounted the notes would become bankrupt, if it had done much business of like nature, and its notes would disappear from circulation. But as long as merchants and manufacturers conduct their operations with a view to realize profits and capital, and not to consume their capital, they will never pay interest on loans for any other purpose than to purchase or produce useful commodities, which commodities become means, when sold, of redeeming the bank notes issued, without necessitating the intervention of coin. The error of the theory we combat arises from omitting to keep in mind the use made of the bank notes or bank credits issued in exchange for the mercantile notes discounted by the banks. The bank notes are represented and will be redeemed by the commodities purchased with them ; and should, from any circumstance, the bank notes not be used for the purchase of commodities, they would remain in the hands of the party obtaining the discount, and would enable him to meet his engagements as well, though to the community not so advantageously, as the commodities he had intended to purchase with them. A constant source of error in all reasonings on transactions in which money intervenes, is looking upon an exchange of commodities against money as the final object of man's desires. It would be, if money were sought for its own sake; but being sought and desired exclusively as means of obtaining, in exchange for it, useful commodities and services, the true effect of any operation can only be ascertained by examining it in its entirety—*i. e.*, by looking not only at what is *given* for money, but also what is *obtained* for it, by the same party, when parted with.

But it is generally supposed that the demand for money by commerce and industry is unlimited, insatiable,* and that the attempt to satisfy this demand invariably leads to over issues, which depreciate the value of the currency, increase the money price of all things, and prevent the exportation of the products of the country.† This is the theory that led to the bank act of 1844, limiting the issues of the Bank of England. Let us examine what truth there is in these assumptions.

Is it true that the demand for money is unlimited, insatiable? The spendthrift, who desires to obtain money as means of securing commodities and services

* "Of money an individual can never have enough. . . . It is plainly, therefore, the merest drivelling to talk about the demand for money being limited by the wants of the public. They have no possible limit." (Encyclopædia Britannica, Money.)

† "If the banks at any time make money more plentiful than it would be if only gold and silver circulated, they diminish its value by increasing its quantity." (Gouge on Banking, p. 18.)

"The banks, by expanding their issues, cause flour, cotton, and other commodities to rise so high at home that they cannot be exported and sold at a profit abroad." (Id., p. 22.)

for his own personal enjoyment, is insatiable in his desire for money; and he alone must have been thought of when the theory was imagined. But commerce and industry never seek money except when it can be profitably employed. They are forced to pay interest on all loans of money obtained by them, and to give what is supposed to be ample security for their repayment at a given day. Self-interest, therefore, constantly induces every one to refuse to borrow money unless it can be used profitably.* Now it is a well-established law of political economy that whenever anything is produced or imported in excess of the wants of the community, or of its ability to pay for it, its price will fall to such a point as will check further production or importation. Here is a natural, proper, and efficient limit to the demand for money, one perfectly in harmony with the interests of the community; and that this limit exists and is operative, is proved by the well-known fact that interest frequently falls to very low rates, not in consequence of the increased volume of the

* "The public do not receive notes from a banker without paying interest for their use; and however low that may be, they will take no more than they absolutely require—nor do they retain notes in their possession beyond what the convenience of trade requires; and, therefore, if issued in excess of that quantity, and if convertible, a portion would be instantly returned upon the issuers. Nor can we conceive any means whatever by which this circulation could be so augmented; and we have deeply to regret that, although such a power on the part of the banks has been taken for granted by most of the writers during the past twelve years, no one has yet attempted to explain by what process it could be accomplished; and we are compelled to think that impressions which gained ground many years since as applicable to an inconvertible currency have been inadvertently associated also with a convertible currency." (Capital, Currency, and Banking, by James Wilson, Esq., M. P., Editor of the London Economist—quoted by Tooke, History of Prices, vol. iii, p. 195.)

currency, but solely from the difficulty of finding, momentarily, a profitable employment for money. In general, the rate of interest, everywhere, at all times, indicates the profit which the employment of money is supposed to yield. This supposed profit is not always realized, but whenever it becomes evident that the anticipated profit is turned into a loss, the demand for money to be employed in the same operations ceases entirely. In moments of embarrassment and panic, when confidence is shaken, the rates of interest are very high, because, then, all kinds of property can be purchased at very low rates, generally much under the cost of production. Everybody then seeks to borrow, and is willing to pay high rates of interest ; one with a view to purchase at the low prices then ruling—another from a desire to avoid the heavy sacrifices that the realization of property, in such moments, invariably entails. In the United States money is generally worth from 7 to 10 per cent., not because it is scarce, but because it can be employed so as to yield a profit over and above those rates of interest. In Europe, if interest is only worth from 3 to 5 per cent., it is simply because the profits arising from its employment there will not permit the payment of higher rates.

## CHAPTER IX.

It is self-evident that, if the theory that the volume of the currency affects prices be true, every rise or fall in the money price of things which proceeds altogether from an alteration in the value of money must affect all things equally—must raise or lower prices everywhere where the currency is used. But such an effect has never yet been known to take place *except with irredeemable government paper money.* No influx of the precious metals, and no issues of bank notes convertible into coin, have ever produced such a result. Much has been said and written on the effect on prices of the influx of the precious metals after the discovery of America. A rise of prices took place in the 17th century. As America had been discovered in 1492, and had furnished a large supply of the precious metals in the 16th and 17th centuries, the rise of prices having followed these events, it was ascribed to them, without much examination of the facts. Now because certain events follow each other, it is not always correct to assert that the anterior event is the cause of those that follow. There is every reason to believe that the rise of prices in the 17th century was entirely the consequence of the increase of industry, commerce, and civilization, which augmented the demand for all the commodities that contributed to man's well being. "No rise of prices can be discovered until 1570, fifty years after the entry of the Spaniards into Mexico, and almost thirty years after the discovery of the Potosi silver mine. The ultimate range of prices was not reached till 1640—and in 1640 and subsequently, the rise of prices was equal to about 200 per cent., while the increase in the whole stock of gold and silver was equal to at least 600 per cent." * Fullarton says: "We observe no such consentaneous movements of prices coinciding with the fluctuations of the bank-note circulation. . . . So little have these variations (in the price of grain) been influenced by the amount of the issues of the Bank of England, that there appears from the investigations of Mr. Tooke to have occurred only one instance within the last half-century in which an increased circulation of notes has coincided with a rise of the price of wheat (and that only a temporary and trifling rise), and one other case in which a reduction of the bank's issues has been simultaneous with a decline in the price of wheat, namely, in 1824 and 1831. . . . The expansions and contractions of the bank-note currency, which under certain circumstances are observed to accompany those fluctuations of prices, are not the *causes*, but the *consequences* of such fluctuations; they do not precede, but follow them." †

* Tooke, History of Prices, vol. vi, p. 232.

† Regulation of Currencies, pp. 98–100.

"The expansion and contraction of bills of exchange, book credits, and of country bank notes, are the consequences, and not the cause, of a rise and fall of prices." (Tooke, History of Prices, vol. i, p. 149.)

"The general depression of credit and of prices, in 1793, was the main

Mr. James Wilson says: "From the beginning of 1841 to 1843 we had an uninterrupted favorable exchange, the bullion in the bank rapidly increased all the time from £3,965,000 to upward of £11,000,000; every means were used which properly could be to increase the circulation; but it fell, during that time, from £35,600,000 to £34,049,000, and during the whole period the prices of commodities generally were sinking lower; and in 1842, the year in which the largest import of gold took place, was the most depressed in prices, and the lowest in the circulation of any during the last thirty years. Nor were the stocks of commodities generally above an average, and the imports were much below an average; and up to this time (April 19, 1848), though bullion has latterly increased to upward of £16,000,000, and the recent efforts of the bank to increase the circulation have proved unavailing, and the prices of all kinds of commodities, even in the absence of any unusual stocks, with some few exceptions, continue unprecedentedly low. The events of the last four years must go far to convince even those who will not exercise the patience to investigate and understand the theory, that a great error has existed in regard to the connection between bank circulation and prices of commodities." *

cause of the contraction of the circulation, and not the contraction of the circulation a cause of the depression." (Tooke, History of Prices, vol. i, p. 197.)

"Mr. Hume, in a debate in the House of Commons, in 1836, said: 'My opinion is, that the quantity of money depends on the rise of prices; and that the rise of prices does not depend on the quantity of money.'" (Id., ib., vol. iii, p. 174.)

* Capital, Currency, and Banking, quoted by Tooke, History of Prices, vol. iii, p. 209.

Mr. Danson says: "Between March and September, 1845, joint-stock speculations, for the immediate investment of capital, were set on foot, involving a larger aggregate amount than had ever before been so involved in the country. The amount, to raise which, for railways alone, the sanction of Parliament was actually applied for in the following session, exceeded £340,000,000; and if we include all the new schemes on which scrips, or letters of allotment, were actually selling in the market at a premium in July, August, and September, 1845, the amount cannot be estimated at less than £500,000,000."

"During those months in which the purchases and sales of railway property were most numerous and extensive, while everybody was buying and selling shares, and the current rate of interest was only 2½ per cent., that portion of the circulating medium which consisted of Bank of England notes was but very slightly, if at all, increased; and it reached its greatest amount when the prices of shares were lowest—when everybody had

"The assumption of the peculiar influence of bank notes on prices, and on the exchanges, is unsustained by fact or argument." (Tooke, History of Prices, vol. iii, p. 156.)

"The balance of payments with nearly all Europe has for about four years past been in favor of this country, and gold has been pouring in till the influx amounts to the unheard-of sum of about fourteen millions sterling. Yet in all this time, has any one heard a complaint of any serious suffering inflicted on the people of the Continent? have prices there been greatly depressed below their ranges in this country? have wages fallen, or have merchants been extensively ruined by the universal depreciation of their stock? There has occurred nothing of the kind. The tenor of commercial and monetary affairs has been everywhere even and tranquil; and in France more particularly, an improving revenue and extended commerce bear testimony to the continued progress of internal prosperity." (Fullarton on the Regulation of Currencies, p. 134.")

6*

ceased to speculate—when the number and amount of current transactions were reduced to the lowest point by discredit, and when the current rate of interest for first-class bills had risen from 2½ to 4½ per cent." *

Tooke says: "Cotton, at the end of May, 1851, was 60 to 70 per cent. below the rates in January 1851, and during the summer great embarrassment and many failures were the consequence. In July, August, and September, there was great depression in the produce markets. The decline of prices of colonial produce was 20 to 30 per cent. The circulation of the Bank of England and of the country banks was, in January, 1850, £29,720,000; in November, 1851, £30,860,000. The highest Bank of England circulation was in July, 1851, £21,400,000, and yet July was among the gloomiest months of the whole year." (Vol. v, pp. 261-266.) "As far as trustworthy evidence can be obtained, there are no facts in the experience of the last nine years which justify the conclusion that in this country the fluctuations of prices, the course of trade, or the increased demand for goods arising out of the large exports to America and Australia, were immediately preceded by or connected with changes in the amount of the aggregate outstanding circulation of bank notes. In other words, all the evidence available to us points distinctly and uniformly to the conclusion that the fluctuations of the bank-note circulation were determined and regulated by the consequences flowing from previous applications of capital and credit in particular modes. . . .

* Extract from a paper read before the Statistical Society of London, in January, 1847—quoted by Tooke, History of Prices, vol. iii, pp. 299, 300.

In a great number of specific instances, it can be shown conclusively, that fluctuations of price of the most important kind, and in the largest markets of the country, took place either without the concurrence of any change whatever in the bank-note circulation, or contemporaneously with the occurrence of a change, the precise opposite of that which are the grounds on which the currency theory is built." (Vol. v, pp. 344, 345.)

"In the nine years, 1848 to 1856, the metallic circulation of the leading commercial nations of the world has been increased by about one third, or say 30 per cent. . . . . It is not true that even an increase by one third of the quantity of metallic money has led to a corresponding increase of general prices; nor, in the case of large groups of commodities, to any increase of price whatever; but on the contrary, that prices have rather sunk to a lower than risen to a higher level." (Vol. vi, pp. 158–194.)

"It is impossible to affirm that the range of general prices has been sensibly raised, by the mere operation in the form of metallic money of even £160,000,000 to £170,000,000 of new gold introduced into the commercial world. All the instances of an important variation in price, comparing 1857 and 1851, admit of being accounted for by circumstances affecting the supply or the demand." (Vol. vi, p. 224.)*

* "How then, let me ask, with all the facilities of communication at present existing, is it possible that the price of the metal can ever fall materially below the minimum (3*l.* 17*s.* 9*d.* at which the Bank of England is obliged to purchase all standard gold bullion tendered to it for sale); or that, with this universal reservoir (the Bank of England) forever open to receive it at a fixed valuation, any considerable portion of the yearly produce of the gold mines should be thrown on the market of the

"I cannot help thinking that there is a lurking impression among the doctrinaires of the currency theory, arising mainly from the use of the term '*issue of paper money*,' which leads them to confound bank notes, strictly convertible into coin, with a compulsory and inconvertible paper currency. . . . But bank notes are issued to those only who, being entitled to demand gold, desire to have bank notes in preference; and it depends upon the particular purposes for which the notes are employed, whether a greater or less quantity is required. The quantity, therefore, is an *effect*, and not a *cause* of demand." (Vol. iii, pp. 175–177.)

Fullarton says: "I deny that we have any evidence of such a redundance of circulating bank notes having ever existed in coincidence with a really convert-

world in such a manner as to occasion its depreciation? . . . However large that surplus may be, after supplying the periodical wants of the other countries of the world for consumption and for coinage, it is obvious that the whole must find its way into the vaults of the Bank of England, there to remain buried, and *wholly inoperative* on prices, till called forth by some new demand for additional circulation. This circumstance, I apprehend, so long as the system shall endure, must continue a perpetual and insuperable obstacle to any action on prices, as measured in gold coin, from the increased productiveness of the mines. It is true that, for every ounce of gold which it thus purchases, the bank may, if that mode of payment be preferred, issue a corresponding amount of notes; . . . but these notes will fare just as all the issues of the bank invariably fare, which are sent into a market having no employment for them. . . . They will fast flow into the bank, in payment of the bills of exchange previously in its hands, as they successively become due, while there will be no vent for its notes in new discounts; and the result of the whole will be, that, at the end of perhaps a week, the bank will find itself with a million more of coin in its coffers, and a million less of securities; so long as the bank has a pound note out on credit, the channel of reflux must remain open, and the bank is utterly impotent to add a superfluous note to the currency." (Fullarton on the Regulation of Currencies, pp. 77–79.)

ible state of the currency, as to raise prices or to cause an efflux of the precious metals, or that such a redundance under such circumstances is possible." * "It is self-evident that bank notes, payable at all times in coin of a definite weight and quality, can never sensibly fall in value below the coin into which they are convertible." † "What has chiefly, I suspect, given currency to the notion that the issues of the Bank of England are in a high degree accessory to the extravagances of the speculative mania, has been the pressure on the Bank of England for discounts, after the malady has reached its concluding stage, *when the excitement has come to a pause*, when the market irrecoverably sinking, discredit spreading rapidly, and payments can no longer be deferred. Then, certainly, if the bank complies with these applications, it must comply with them by an issue of notes, for notes constitute the only instrumentality through which the bank is in the practice of lending its credits. But those notes are not intended to circulate, nor do they circulate. There is no more demand for circulation than there was before. On the contrary, the rapid decline of prices which the case in supposition presumes, would necessarily contract the demand for circulation." ‡

"Applications to the bank for extended discounts occur rarely, if ever, in the origin or progress of extensive speculations in commodities. These are entered into for the most part, if not entirely, in the first instance, on credit, for the length of term usual in the

* On the Regulation of Currencies, p. 26.

† Ib., p. 117.

‡ Ib., p. 105.

several trades; thus entailing on the parties no immediate necessity for borrowing so much as may be wanted for the purpose beyond their own available capital. And if the events fully justify the grounds on which the speculative transactions were entered into (thus admitting of sales for consumption in time to replace the capital embarked), there is no unusual demand for borrowed capital to sustain them. The term speculation, in its obnoxious sense, is not, in such cases, applied to the transactions; and the parties engaged have the credit of superior sagacity. It is only when, by the vicissitudes of political events, or of the seasons, or other adventitious circumstances, the forthcoming supplies are found to exceed the computed rate of consumption, and a fall of prices ensues, that an increased demand for capital (credit ?) takes place; the market rate of interest then rises, and increased applications are made to the Bank of England for discount."*

It is said that the value of money, and particularly of paper money which has no intrinsic value, is maintained by limiting its quantity.† This theory is based on the fact that when anything used as money exists in greater quantity than is necessary to effect the daily occurring exchanges, it has a tendency to fall in

* Tooke, History of Prices, vol. iii, pp. 125, 126.

† "Whatever may be the *material* of the money of any country, . . and however destitute it may be of all intrinsic value, it is yet possible, by sufficiently limiting its quantity, to raise its value in exchange to any conceivable extent." (McCulloch, Money, chap. ii.)

"There can be no doubt that by sufficiently limiting its quantity, a currency, though destitute of intrinsic worth, may be made to circulate on a level with gold and silver, *or higher, if it be desired.*" (Encyclopædia Britannica, Money.)

its exchangeable value because persons will not retain it idle, as it then produces no income, and may depreciate still further. But of all currencies, a paper currency issued by solvent banks or individuals is the one least liable to experience this result ; in fact, it cannot experience it at all. An irredeemable government paper money is subject to this depreciation, because when issued in excess of the wants of the community, there being no way by which the quantity in circulation can be diminished, every one attempts to get rid of it on the best possible terms, precisely as with commodities. And if coin exists in excess of its profitable use, it must be exported, or lie idle, rendering no service, producing no income. There is therefore also a tendency, in such cases, to get rid of coin on the best possible terms. But not so with bank notes issued by sound institutions or solvent individuals. They need never be kept idle on hand, lent out at a low rate of interest, or exchanged on onerous terms for commodities or other property ; because, being all issued in the form of loans, the persons who borrowed them of the banks, as soon as they find they can no longer employ them profitably, many always return them to the banks, and thus stop the interest they pay for them.* There cannot, there-

* "Try then the bank notes by the same tests, and see if the principles which determine a rise of prices, in the case of a more abundant influx of the precious metals, or of the redundant issues of a conventional currency, can have the least application to them. There is this broad and clear distinction between all currencies of value and currencies of credit, that the quantity of the former is in no degree regulated by the public demand, whereas the quantity of the latter is regulated by nothing else. The gold which is once smelted and converted into coin, can never be returned again into the mine: there it is, a permanent and irrevocable addition to the

fore, be a redundancy of bank notes, when issued by well-managed institutions, that only issue them on good security.* The possibility of increasing and de-

stock of money in the world. . . . Still more decidedly have the conventional issues of government all the characteristics of a forced currency; . . . even after the notes have become depreciated, the law compels the private creditor to accept them in satisfaction of his claims; and the government having no better money to offer, the only alternative left to its creditors and dependants is to take this or none. Bank notes, on the other hand, are never issued but on the demand of the recipient parties. New gold coin and new conventional notes are introduced into the market by being made the medium of *payments.* Bank notes, on the contrary, are never issued but *on loans*, and an equal amount of notes must be returned into the bank whenever the loan becomes due. Bank notes never, therefore, can clog the market by their redundance, nor afford a motive to any one to pay them away at a reduced value in order to get rid of them. The banker has only to take care that they are lent on sufficient security, and the reflux and the issue will, in the long run, always balance each other. However prone individuals may be to abuse at times the facility of borrowing, no merchant can ever desire to keep by him a larger sum in bank notes than is indispensably necessary for his payments; and if any one were disposed to indulge in so unprofitable a fancy, it would be a matter of not the slightest importance to any other than himself, for, in so far as the public are concerned, notes which are not in use are the same as if they were not in existence. Those notes cannot be obtained from a banker but by paying interest for the use of them, nor can they be obtained at all but for very short periods, at the expiration of which they must be replaced. Their circulation must always be strictly limited by the wants of those who have value or security to offer for them. And so limited, there can be no redundance; no holder of them can ever be placed in the same predicament with the importers of a double supply of bullion, or the recipients of a forced issue of government paper, who have no means of turning these acquisitions to use but by submitting to part with them at a reduced value." (Fullarton on the Regulation of Currencies, pp. 64, 65.)

"Mr. Whitmore, Governor of the Bank of England, on his examination before the Bullion Committee of 1810, said: 'The bank notes would revert to us if there was a redundancy in circulation, as no one would pay interest for a bank note that he did not want to make use of.'" (Tooke, History of Prices, vol. i, p. 160.)

* "It may rest with the banker to issue, but it is the public which cir-

creasing each day the volume of the currency, exactly in accordance with the amount of the operations which the currency facilitates, instead of being injurious, is one of the great advantages which bank notes offer over every other kind of money. It is very uncertain, and very difficult to ascertain, what is the limit to the profitable employment of money. Neither legislators nor bankers should attempt to fix this limit. The main duty of the banker is to see that he loans only on undoubted security, and for such periods of time as he feels confident will not inconvenience himself. The borrowers are the only proper persons to decide what employment shall be made of the money, or what may be the profit it will yield them. Money applied to consumption may be injurious to the community; but money applied to the production, importation, or

culates; and without the concurrent action of the public, neither the power nor the will to issue can avail. Both the metropolitan and the country circulations are subject to certain periodical floods and ebbs from regularly recurring causes, over which the issuing bodies have no control, and which are found to be of little if any effect beyond the immediate range of the circumstances in which they originate. It is well known, that at the quarterly periods, when the public dividends fall in course of payment, the Bank of England adds regularly from a fifth to two fifths to the amount of its issues. Has any one ever heard of an instance in which any of these great periodical expansions of the bank circulation have, in any sensible degree, disturbed markets or caused a general rise of prices? Nothing of the kind. . . . Such is the elasticity with which the general circulation throws off the superfluous load which encumbers it, that the surplus notes are usually returned into the bank, and the currency restored to its average level, within a few weeks after the recurrence of each quarterly period. This effect is uniformly produced by a reduction of the demand, on the part of the public, for accommodations from the bank by way of discount or loan,—a reduction which follows, with immediate and striking regularity, every such extraordinary augmentation of the bank issues." (Fullarton on the Regulation of Currencies, p. 86.)

exchange of commodities can never greatly injure the community, whatever be the result to the individuals making these operations; for increased production diminishes prices—low prices diminish production—diminished production increases prices—higher prices stimulate production. Thus we have constantly action and reaction—harmony resulting from the antagonism of forces, which appears to be the universal system that controls so harmoniously all created things.

But if limiting the issues of paper currency really increased its value, how injurious and how unjust would be such a measure as the limitation of the issues of the Bank of England to 14 millions! Every day increases the population of all countries, whilst the enormous development of industry and wealth in consequence of the invention of machinery, the greater and greater division of labor, and the increasing intelligence of the laborers, increases production and exchanges still more rapidly than population. It is evident that an amount of currency amply sufficient for the exchanges of 1844, may be totally insufficient to effect the exchanges of 1864; and, therefore, the limitation of the issues of bank notes, if the theory that this increases their value were correct, would each day increase the value of money, and reduce the value of commodities and services, *although no change should take place in the relative proportion between the supply and the demand; in fact, even if the supply had moderately diminished in proportion to the demand.* Can it be that man can thus counteract a great beneficial natural law? No, thank God, this cannot be done, for otherwise we should constantly see the masses still more frequently deprived than they are now of the results of their labor, at the will, and for the benefit of the intriguing few who succeed in obtaining possession of the government, *i. e.* of the power to enact human laws. *The volume of the currency has no durable effect on prices.* It would, if all things could only be exchanged by means of money ; but as that is not the case, the currency is only an instrument that facilitates exchanges, but does not control prices. Mr. Wm. Newmarch, in an address at Manchester in September, 1861, said : "It has been proved by evidence so extensive and various that we may well claim for it the force of demonstration, that fluctuations in the amount of a paper circulation strictly convertible into coin, does not govern prices at all, but that prices are governed by supply and demand, and by operations of capital and credit ; that bank notes are no more than the small change of the ledger, and that the phenomena which are really worth attention are not infinitesimal fluctuations in the amount of bank notes, but changes in the rate of interest." *

But, unfortunately, although the theory that limiting the quantity of the currency increases its value is not true in principle, it is true in some exceptional cases ; and the theory, as long as admitted and acted on, does immense injury to the best interests of the community ; for, whenever the community obtain a certain supply of currency and adapt their operations to this amount, the contraction that subsequently takes place either in consequence of legal restrictions to bank issues, like in the case of the Bank of England, or in consequence of the ignorance of the true laws governing paper money on the

* Journal of the Statistical Society of London, December, 1861.

part of the issuers, as is universally the case in the United States, is perfectly ruinous to the commercial and industrial interests, because the deprivation of the indispensable means of exchanging commodities and meeting engagements, invariably creates panics; leads to forced sales of property at ruinous rates; destroys credit, and ends by arresting and disorganizing industry for a longer or shorter period of time. Such a contraction of the currency, and the subsequent rise of prices which follows after confidence is reëstablished and the currency once more increased to an amount sufficient for the exchanges then taking place, give a certain appearance of truth to the theory that the volume of the currency regulates prices. But it is evident that these incessant expansions and contractions of the currency, without regard to the wants of the community, and their injurious effects, are not the consequences of the use of paper money, but solely of its abuse, of the ignorance of those who control the issues of paper money. If an instrument of any kind be beneficial, how can it be injurious to increase the number in use, as long as those who are to use them ask and pay for them? Suppose it were asserted that increasing the number of ploughs decreased their value, and that, therefore, to protect the interests of the community, it was necessary to limit the number of ploughs in use. Could this be beneficial to any one but the present holders of ploughs, who thereby would be benefited by the increase of their value? Exactly so with paper money. By making those who obtain paper money from the issuers, give security for its return and pay interest for its use until returned, the demand for paper money is certain to be limited at all times to the amount really useful to the borrowers. And if any given amount be useful to the commercial and industrial interests, it cannot be injurious to any portion of humanity ; for it is now clearly established by political economy, that under perfect liberty, anything really beneficial to a portion, is beneficial to the whole of humanity. The contrary doctrine arises, invariably, from looking only at the first effects, and omitting all consideration of the subsequent, ulterior, effects of any measure.

It is generally supposed that the redemption of paper issues in specie is the best guarantee against over issues. This is what is called in England "the banking principle," * which supposes that this is necessary to maintain the value of a paper currency on a par with the currency of other nations with which commodities are exchanged. It is supposed that whenever the paper issues become redundant they reduce the value of the currency, which leads to an exportation of the precious metals from the country whose circulation is excessive, and this then leads to the presentation of bank notes to obtain specie to meet the export demand, until the equilibrium of both volume and value be re-established. Here we have again the theory that every increase in the volume of the currency decreases its value. The true and only advantage of the converti-

* "That the purposes of a mixed circulation of coin and paper were sufficiently answered, as long as the coin was perfect and the paper constantly convertible into coin, and that the only evils to be guarded against by regulation were those attending suspension of payment and insolvency of the banks. This is what is understood in general terms as the 'banking principle,' and is that upon which our system of currency is constructed and conducted." (Tooke, History of Prices, vol. iii, p. 167.)

bility of paper money into coin, on demand, is that, as the banks, wherever they exist, become the reservoirs of the specie reserves of the entire community, as long as the precious metals are considered the only true and desirable wealth, and paper money only performs the functions of money within limited districts, the forced convertibility becomes necessary as means of overcoming the dislike of the banks to part with the coveted metals when they become indispensable to commerce as means of supplying some want or desire beyond the means offered by the exports of commodities for the moment. Were bank notes universally accepted as money, and the precious metals used simply as commodities, the exports of gold and silver would be seen with as great satisfaction as the exports of all other commodities by means of which we obtain, in return, the objects of our wants or desires. Under our present system, the moment commerce requires specie as means of supplying the wants or desires of the community, instead of loaning it against ample security, precisely as they do their notes, the banks immediately call in the loans and notes indispensable to the operations of the community,* merely with a view to arrest the exports of coin, although the only utility of coin is to meet precisely such emergencies. The community are thus not only attempted to be deprived of the use of the precious metals brought into the country solely by means of their industry and intelligence, but are further deprived of the

* "Bankers, though they cannot increase their issues above the level prescribed by prices, *have it always in their power to lower them to any given point*, or to withdraw them, if they think fit, altogether." (Fullarton on the Regulation of Currencies, p. 107.)

instruments indispensable to the local exchanges of commodities and services.* The invariable result is an immense momentary reduction, if not a total cessation of the production of commodities, although the community are in as great need of them as ever, and possess the same ample means as ever to remunerate the producers by other services useful to the latter.

Nothing that will arrest the exportations of the products of a country, while there is a foreign demand for them, can produce a rise of prices, as long as the products exist in excess of the local wants. Whenever, from any cause, the foreign demand ceases whilst stocks are in excess of the local demand, prices will fall until the foreign demand recommences or the production is diminished, because merchants rarely purchase commodities to hold them for future wants, but almost always to supply immediate wants. Commerce is not speculation—it is the constant supply of immediate wants. "It will be found that in almost every instance of a drain of bullion, the drain does not commence until after a considerable foreign debt has been already created, and all available means of discharging it through the ordinary course of traffic have been exhausted."† "The *scarcity*

* "When we come to a drain of gold to meet an unavoidable want, there must be some means of avoiding measures by which the commerce of the country will be dislocated. That commerce is carried on almost entirely on a system of credit. If you drive it to a ready money system, you at once paralyze it in the manufacturing districts. . . . How can the mercantile interests carry on the export trade, which must be conducted on credit, when all accommodation is refused them? The country has exported £700,000 of gold, and the effect of this export has been to destroy property to the extent of one hundred millions." (Speech of Thomas Baring, Esq., in the House of Commons, 10th May, 1847, on the crisis of 1847. Alison's History of Europe, vol. viii, p. 101, American edition.)

† Fullarton on the Regulation of Currencies, p. 130.

and (consequent) dearness of native productions is an infallible cause of the export of specie from a country; and an already existing abundant supply of foreign productions of all sorts is a certain cause of the import of specie into a country. On the contrary, when native productions are cheap and abundant, it will cause an importation of bullion; and when foreign productions are scarce and dear, it will cause an export of bullion." * This is just as true of a country where a forced irredeemable paper money circulates, as of one whose currency is entirely metallic, or partly metallic and partly bank notes convertible into coin on demand. Wherever a forced paper money circulates, every depreciation of the paper money is accompained by a corresponding rise in the rates of the foreign exchanges. This rise in the foreign exchanges compensates, to the foreigners, the rise in the price of commodities, which, therefore, cost no more to them than when prices were lower in a sound currency. Exports thus continue as before the depreciation of the currency—in fact, with a depreciated currency, the exports often increase temporarily, in consequence of the rise of the foreign exchanges, as this becomes a great temptation to export commodities in the hope of avoiding a portion of the rise in the exchanges. Commerce never moves the precious metals if it can be avoided, because operations in them offer little or no compensation for the trouble and risk they occasion. †

* Macleod, Theory and Practice of Banking, vol. i, p. 304.

† "The cause of bullion being imported is either that the price of goods is so *low* in England, and so *high* in the foreign markets, as to tempt foreigners to send here to buy goods, or that the price of goods is so high

Drains of specie for export are invariably caused by purchases abroad of a greater amount of commodities than the value of the commodities exported at the moment. A drain of specie can never be of long duration, because commerce maintains a constant equilibrium between all nations both as to the value and the supply of all things. If the purchases abroad have been of articles of necessity, like food, to supply the deficit of bad harvests, they must continue as long as the wants of the community are unsatisfied; but bad harvests produce high prices for food, and low prices for everything else, because the additional amount that has to be expended for food must be withdrawn from some other consumption formerly indulged in, and low prices for all articles but food soon attract a foreign demand which arrests the drain of specie. If the purchases abroad have been of articles of luxury, which can be easily dispensed with, there must be an over importation when the liquidation of the purchases requires an exportation of coin, and this soon corrects itself by the losses invariably entailed upon the importers by importations beyond the wants or means of the community. It must never be forgotten that every one who parts with coin,

in the foreign market and so low in England, that nothing but specie can be sent in payment of goods exported from England.

"The cause of bullion being exported from England is that there is some great and pressing demand for some article in this country, and other commodities are so scarce and dear that they cannot be exported with a profit, or that the article is required in such quantities that the foreigner cannot consume our goods (which we should prefer to send in payment) fast enough, and so specie must be sent, and the greater the difference in price the greater will be the drain of bullion; or that other markets are already overstocked with our productions, which are depressed below their market value there" (Macleod, Theory and Practice of Banking, vol. i, p. 309.)

does so to obtain, in exchange, something he prefers to coin. Now should the exchange of coin for commodities, by individuals, ever be prevented? If not, why attempt to stop the exports of coin, which only represent individual exchanges of coin for foreign commodities? * All efforts to arrest the exportation of coin are simply an attempt to enforce the theory that the only true and desirable wealth is gold and silver. Is it not safe and proper to allow every owner of coin to dispose of it as he may judge most conducive to his well being? He obtained the coin by giving something, in exchange, of equal value. When he thus acquires it, is it not his inherent right to do whatever he pleases with it? Self-interest will ever prevent him from parting with it except in exchange for something which he *prefers* to coin —if he is benefited by the exchange, the nation cannot be injured, because the well being of a nation depends on the well being of the individuals composing the nation.

There is nothing so absurd and groundless as the fear of an inadequate supply of the precious metals as long as commerce is left unfettered by legislation. "Gold is easily transported from one country to another. . . . Owing to the great facilities of communication in modern times, a very slight discrepancy of value is instantly corrected by a stream of exportation. . . . A military emergency, compelling a sudden export to an army abroad, or very sudden and extensive orders for mercan-

* "I really know not why such enormous stores of coin are to be hoarded up at so vast an expense, if they are to be at all times inexorably withheld from the public, whatever be the urgency of the need." (Fullarton on the Regulation of Currencies, p. 150.)

tile purchases in foreign countries, might for the moment produce a considerable diminution of the coin in a nation which held no reserves in bankers' hands; but the vacuum and the inconvenience would be of brief duration. Gold would flow in on every side, so long as people had commodities wherewith to buy it. The horror which the theorists inculcate of a deficiency of gold is simply preposterous; there is probably no other commodity, the scarcity of which would produce so little inconvenience, or would be so rapidly remedied. A scarcity of cotton would, indeed, be a subject for grave alarm; for how could it be supplied? But a deficiency of gold would at once cause it to pour in from the reservoir of the whole world; bankers who had pledged themselves to pay gold, and merchants who owe debts abroad, being the only persons who would incur any real loss; and that would, at the utmost, be trifling. A small premium on the value of the metal would bring in any supply that could be wanted. In truth, this horror of a scarcity of this particular article above that of any other, *is a mere relic of the unscientific confusion of a short supply of a commodity with the inability of an indebted banker to repay his creditors the capital which he has lost.* . . . A premium of sixpence a sovereign, or at the most a shilling, would draw torrents of gold upon England from all the world, and would restore the whole of the sixteen millions of gold at the bank, if it had all taken wing, for some £400,000 or £800,000 at most. Why, reckoning interest at five per cent., it costs the nation the larger of these sums annually to keep cellars at the bank full of gold. . . . *Of all wants, there is none which is so easily and so certainly supplied as gold.* . . . India and China obtain as much silver as they can pay for with their products. Is England, England rich in every store of manufactured and universally desired wealth, unable to do as much? Has Adam Smith taught in vain? and is the absurd doctrine of a favorable balance of trade, of the flowing in of a redundant and useless commodity, not yet exploded?"

"But how, then, is the existence of this strange delusion about gold to be explained? Partly by the old mercantile theory, of which it is a remnant; partly by ignorance of the science of currency; but most of all by the universal and natural feeling of the banking trade, especially of the Bank of England. It is a serious part of their business to undertake to provide gold on demand. Every banker in London, including the Bank of England, is bound by law to repay all his liabilities, whether of notes or deposits, in gold on demand. The business, therefore, of providing gold when wanted, falls on them; it is a duty annexed to the profit of their calling. No wonder, therefore, that they are always nervous as to having gold enough to meet all possible demands on them; no wonder that they preach that vast heaps of stored-up gold, it matters not how useless, constitute a very satisfactory state of things. . . . But it is a wonder that political economists should have chosen to identify the banking interest of the Bank of England with the interest of the whole community; that they should have persuaded themselves that there was any greater harm in dear gold than in dear corn, dear cotton, or dear sugar."

"The terror felt for drains of gold and low (high)

exchanges is almost too absurd to be seriously dealt with. They signify only that gold is being exported; and why not rejoice over its export as much as over that of Manchester bales? Gold is sent out only to bring in a more desirable commodity—a serviceable, in exchange for an unserviceable article. A cargo of cotton or wool is, as a general rule, an arrival far more deserving of welcome than one of gold; and city articles of the press would show more understanding of the matter, if, instead of enumerating the ounces which come from Australia to England—for the most part, too, only in transit to some other country—they would publish the supplies which are brought in of raw material for the great workshops of English industry. If these supplies were to fail, great indeed would be the ruin; but, if gold were scarce for a while, what would be the harm? . . . Scarce gold must be paid for at a high rate. Granted; but the question ultimately is this: whether it would cost more to buy it at a dearer rate occasionally when scarce, or to invest large portions of capital uselessly, in keeping up expensive accumulations of it, for the sole purpose of preventing it from ever being scarce."*

The precious metals, being universally accepted in exchange for commodities and services, imperceptibly became the representatives of commodities and services, by which they are constantly redeemed, and thus maintained current among all those who desire commodities and services, which means humanity at large. Every man seeks money because it has become, like Aladdin's lamp, the efficient means of obtaining, at any moment,

* What is Money? (North British Review, November, 1861.)

everything he may desire.* The ignoring of this transformation of the precious metals from commodities into counters, into representatives of, or orders on, all commodities and services—the belief that gold and silver still circulate as money on account of their intrinsic value, of the value in themselves, as it is sometimes called, leads to the doctrine called in England "the currency principle:" that paper money performs successfully the functions of money solely because it is, or should be, the representative of coin actually in the vaults of the institutions or individuals that issue it. The ultra, logical partisans of this doctrine naturally insist that all issues of paper that do not represent an equivalent amount of coin, idle in the vaults of the issuers, ready to redeem the paper issues, are injurious, because they depreciate the value of the currency by increasing its volume. Here we have, once more, the doctrine that every addition to the existing stock of money diminishes its exchangeable value. But neither the volume of the precious metals, nor the volume of the mixed currency of coin and paper money issued by banks to whom it can be returned when no longer needed, ever has been, or ever will be, the true measure of value of all things produced by the labor of man, because currency never has been, and certainly never will be hereafter, the sole means of obtaining those things. If banks at the present day, like the old banks of Amsterdam and of Hamburgh, were merely the de-

* The alchemists of old sought to transmute commodities into gold. We, more intelligent in regard to the true services that can be obtained from things, constantly transform the precious metals into commodities and services.

positories, the safekeepers, of coin, for the benefit of the holders of the notes issued to an equivalent amount, they would render but very trifling services to humanity; services not worth the cost of the machinery required to render them. It is because the modern banks replace successfully coin by paper, as an instrument for effecting exchanges—because they replace capital, which it requires laborious efforts to produce, by credit, the active and obedient offspring of intelligence and probity—physical efforts by mental efforts, the true process of all human progress—that they have been the source of the great benefits man has already derived from them. Some men, fortunately declining in number each day, believe that the introduction of machinery and of steam has been injurious to humanity because they diminish the labor required to produce certain results; and that, as labor is the true source of wealth, it follows that every diminution in the necessary employment of labor is injurious to society at large. These men forget that labor is necessary and desirable only on account of the results it produces; that if the desired results can be obtained with less effort and in greater profusion by the gratuitous natural forces placed at our disposal by the beneficent Giver of all things, it liberates labor from its former efforts, which then become unnecessary, without diminishing man's enjoyments, and permits him to secure new enjoyments and new sources of future progress by the application of the liberated labor to new occupations. Exactly so with money. If we are liberated from the necessity of using the former expensive instruments of exchanges, in consequence of their being replaced by a gratuitous instrument, it liberates labor and capital, which can then be turned to good account in other pursuits that will add to our present enjoyments and future progress.

Mr. Huskisson said, in 1810: "It is of the essence of money to possess *intrinsic value.* Paper currency has obviously no intrinsic value: a promissory note, under whatever form or from whatever source it may come, *represents* value. It does so, inasmuch as it is an undertaking to pay in money the sum for which it is issued. The money or coin of a country is so much of its capital. Paper currency is no portion of the capital of a country. It is so much circulating credit. . . . Both money, however, and paper promissory of money, are common measures and representatives of the value of all commodities. But money alone is the universal equivalent. Paper currency is the representative of that money."* We have here, in a few words, the principal errors of the ultra bullionists, who imagined the "currency principle" and the act of 1844. "Money (coin) is capital." We think it is not capital, but only the representative of capital, as long as used as money. To perform the functions of capital, and become subject to the laws regulating capital, it must be demonetized by being melted. "Money must possess intrinsic value." We think we have shown that this is entirely unnecessary. "Paper money does not possess intrinsic value, therefore it cannot perform the functions of money." Experience shows conclusively it can, most successfully, perform the functions of money. No people that have once used paper money have ever long given up its use. "Paper money circulates as money

* The Question concerning the Depreciation of our Currency stated and examined—quoted by Tooke, History of Prices, vol. vi, p. 618.

because it is a promise to pay coin, and, therefore, represents coin." We say paper money circulates, not because it represents *coin,* but because it represents *commodities and services.* Paper money is redeemed, not in coin, but by payments to the issuers in liquidation of loans of paper money. It is redeemed by commodities and services, in exchange for which the bank notes are transferred, by those who receive them from the banks, to those who have to pay to the banks. Paper money cannot be redeemed in coin if it be issued in excess of the coin in the hands of the issuers.* "Money is the equivalent of all things." No, it is not; it is a mere representative of all other things. Huskisson claims that paper money is the representative of coin. If that be correct, it must be because paper money is eventually to be redeemed in coin. Then why is not money of every kind the representative of commodities and services, since these must constantly redeem it to give currency to money of any kind, for money is only used as means of obtaining all things useful or desired. Bullionists, however, will not admit that money represents commodities and services, because that admission overthrows all their theories. Huskisson admits that paper money is a measure of value, and he states very correctly that it is circulating credit. Bank notes are undoubtedly credit in its most convenient form.

* "Bank notes are regarded by some as representatives of specie. But for every silver dollar they have in their vaults, some of the banks have two paper dollars in circulation, some three, some five, some eight, and some thirteen. Bank notes cannot represent that which the banks have not, and which is not in the country." (Gouge on Banking, p. 20.)

## CHAPTER X.

Paper money, as yet, is far from being the perfect money it will, some day, become. Up to the present time it is far too much controlled and hampered by legislation, and the natural laws that govern it so perfectly are not yet sufficiently known to permit us to derive all the benefits its use will, eventually, confer. Notwithstanding all the advantages offered by paper money, it performs, as yet, but a portion of the required functions of money. It only aids the exchanges of commodities and services within restricted limits. For exchanges between distant points the precious metals are still greatly used. The reason of this is that paper money does not yet inspire universal confidence, without which nothing can properly perform the functions of money, and the issues of each institution are only known in a restricted circle, in the more or less immediate vicinity of the locality of the institutions that issue it. But each day rapidly increases the general intelligence, the intercourse between nations, and, consequently, the universal knowledge of the institutions of all countries. Steam, railroads, and the electric telegraph, not only supply our wants, but annihilate ignorance, distances, and time. We are rapidly progressing toward the moment when paper money will become a perfect money in every respect. It will then become the universal instrument for effecting the exchanges of the entire globe. The precious metals will then be abandoned as money, and left exclusively to the arts; and history will speak of the times when they were used as money precisely as we now do of the dark ages, when cattle and iron were used for that purpose. Universal intelligence and universal probity, the conviction that deception, dishonesty, and idleness are unprofitable, are required, above all, to attain this desirable result; and this, to pessimists, will appear as impossible as to replace the precious metals by paper money. But when we contrast the present with the past, can we doubt the future moral as well as physical progress of humanity? Dr. Bowring stated at a meeting of the Society of Political Economy, of Paris, that in the county in which he was born, in Scotland, two out of three prisons that existed were no longer used, *theft having become an unprofitable occupation.* Already the notes of the Bank of England can be disposed of, more or less readily, throughout most civilized countries, in consequence of the large capital and well-established and well-deserved confidence in the prudent and intelligent management of that institution. And yet it is far, very far, from being a model bank, owing to its close connection with the state, to its being a monopoly, and to the numerous injurious restrictions imposed on its operations.* Without liberty and with-

* "Lord King, in 1826, said that 'if the purpose was to erect an establishment to do mischief, they would erect it on the very principles of the

out competition, nothing can approach perfection. This cannot be repeated too often.*

Some of the facts connected with the history of the Bank of England will throw much light on the subject of paper money.

The Bank of England has now existed over a century and a half: during this period of time, war after war has devastated the world ; nation after nation has been driven to national bankruptcy ; and yet the bank exists more firmly than ever. The suspension of specie payments by the bank in 1696 and 1797 was the consequence of its connection with the state (to which it had loaned its entire capital), and not of its advances to commerce and industry ; and during those suspensions, the public never ceased to accept readily its notes in payment of services and commodities, even though they could not be converted into specie except at a premium. Would its notes have been thus received during the suspension of specie payments, if paper money, as many persons suppose, is, or should be, a mere representative of the precious metals?

bank. They would give it a monopoly, remove from it all fear of rivalry, and connect it with the Government.' " (Macleod, Theory and Practice of Banking, vol. ii, p. 254.)

"The great law of nature in the industrial world is *free trade*. There is nothing more certain in all the range of science, than that exclusive privileges in commerce are great violations of natural right. Trading monopolies are moral crimes. When Parliament sold to the Bank of England the exclusive monopoly of banking, it sold what it had no right to sell." (Macleod, Theory and Practice of Banking, vol. ii, p. 517.)

* "The admirable effect of freedom is finely exhibited in the situation of the New England banks in 1837, after a period of unparalleled speculation, during which they *could not* increase their loans to more than forty-three per cent. beyond their capital." (H. C. Carey, The Credit System, p. 113.)

The suspension of 1696 was, in a great measure, caused by the undertaking of the bank to have recoined the depreciated silver coins then in circulation, which, in consequence of clipping and wear, had become reduced, on an average, 25 per cent. below the standard. For this purpose the bank had received, and then held, a large amount of this depreciated silver, which it could not use until recoined. The difficulties of the bank were soon, however, overcome by the aid of Government. Had the bank not loaned its entire capital to the state, the depreciated coin in its vaults could not have caused a suspension. During this first suspension of specie payments, the notes of the bank were as low as 25 per cent. discount, but this was at a moment when exchequer bills and treasury bonds were at 40, 50, and even 60 per cent. discount! Can there be a better evidence of the superiority of bank notes over government paper issues?

Previous to 1759, the bank issued no notes below £20, but in that year it commenced to issue notes of £15 and £10. In 1794 the bank first issued notes under £10.

In 1720, after the collapse of the South Sea Company, and again in 1745, in consequence of the successes of the Pretender in Scotland, the bank experienced severe runs, which nearly drained it of its coin: on both of these occasions the bank, to gain time, paid its notes in sixpences and shillings, blocked up its doors with its own friends, who returned the coin they received, and thus succeeded in weathering the danger. We have here convincing proofs of the propriety of maintaining specie payments as long as any coin remains in the vaults of a bank. In most cases, if the bank be in a sound condition, the drain ceases before the coin is exhausted.

"In 1793, on the execution of the king of France, the British Government expelled the French ambassador, and the Convention instantly declared war. . . . This gave a shock to credit, which was already staggering. On the 15th of February, a house of considerable magnitude, deep in corn speculations, failed, and on the 19th, the bank refused the paper of Lane, Son & Fraser, who stopped next morning, to the amount of nearly £1,000,000, involving a great number of other respectable houses. In the mean time, the panic spread to the bankers. Beginning at Newcastle, the panic immediately spread throughout the country. It was computed that there were nearly four hundred country banks at that time ; of these three hundred were much shaken, and upward of one hundred stopped payment. . . . All these circumstances naturally produced a demand on the Bank of England for support and discounts. But the bank, being thoroughly alarmed, resolved to contract its issues. Bankruptcies multiplied with frightful rapidity. The Government urged the bank to come forward and support credit, but the directors resolutely declined. When the bank adopted this perverse course, universal failure seemed imminent. Sir John Sinclair, on the 16th of April, suggested an issue of exchequer bills. The subject was referred to a committee of the House of Commons, who recommended an issue of £5,000,000. No sooner was the act passed than a large sum of money, £70,000, was sent down to Manchester and Glasgow, on the strength of the exchequer bills which were not yet issued. This unexpected supply coming so much earlier than was expected, operated like magic, and had a greater effect in restoring credit than ten times the sum could have had at a later period. The whole amount of exchequer bills advanced was £2,202,000, the whole of which was repaid; two only of the parties assisted became bankrupts; all the others were ultimately solvent, and in many instances possessed of great property."

"The success of the measure was perfect and complete. The contemporary writers all bear witness to the extraordinary effects produced. The bullion committee of 1810, in their report, warmly approved of it, and especially cite it as an illustration of a principle which they laid down, *that an enlarged accommodation is the true remedy for that occasional failure of confidence* in the country districts to which our system of paper credit is unavoidably exposed." *

"The position of the Bank was:

| | Circulation. | Bullion. | Discounts. |
|---|---|---|---|
| 1785, | £5,923,090 | | £4,973,926 |
| 1789, | 11,121,800 | £8,645,860 | 2,035,901 |
| August, 1791, | 11,672,320 | 8,055,510 | 1,898,640 |
| Febr'y, 1793, | 11,888,910 | 4,010,680 | 6,456,041 |

"We find here that the bank had fully kept up its circulation, and largely increased its discounts, while it supplied the country with a large amount of gold; *and yet the prices of almost all commodities were lower in* 1793 *than they had been in the two years preceeding,* and the price of wheat was below the average of the three years previous to the harvest of 1791; 3 per cent. consols had fallen from 96 in 1792 to 72 in 1793, at which price the first loan in preparation for the war was

* Macleod, Theory and Practice of Banking, vol. ii, pp. 69–74.

contracted." * We find here certainly no evidence to maintain the theory that the volume of the currency affects prices.

"The catastrophe of 1797 began in 1795. The spring of 1795 was very cold and backward, the summer wet and stormy, and the harvest unusually late. Under these circumstances, wheat, which was 55*s.* in in January, reached 108*s.* in August. The same scarcity was general throughout Europe and America. Mr. Pitt, in 1793, having obtained from Parliament an act permitting the bank to make advances to Government in anticipation of the taxes, obtained large advances in 1795 to aid him in the foreign subsidies, which, in that year alone, amounted to £6,253,140. All this produced a large foreign drain of bullion, and that of the bank in December, 1796, was reduced to £2,508,000, when a drain set in more severe than ever. In December, the French expedition under Hoche sailed, but fortunately it was dispersed by a tempest; only a few straggling vessels reached Ireland in the last week of December, the rest putting back to France. This terrible menace produced a continual demand for gold for Ireland. A French frigate went into one of the Welsh harbors and landed 1,200 men. This created a perfect panic among the farmers. On Saturday, 18th of February, 1797, being market day, the farmers, who at that time of year had the principal part of their rents (crops ?) in their hands, actuated by the terror of an immediate invasion, hurried into Newcastle the produce of their farms, which they sold at very low prices, and immediately rushed to the different banks to demand specie. Seeing

* Tooke, History of Prices, vol. i, pp. 194–197.

this universal panic, the banks, by agreement, stopped payment on the Monday.

"On the 21st of February, the state of the bank became so alarming that the directors resolved that the time had come when they must make a communication to the Government. The directors had used the most violent efforts to contract their loans. On the 21st of January, they were £10.550,830; on the 25th of February, they were £8,640,250; a reduction of nearly £2,000,000. In order to meet their payments, persons were obliged to sell their stock of all descriptions, at an enormous sacrifice. The 3 per cents fell to 51, and other stock in proportion.

"A meeting of the cabinet was held on Sunday at Whitehall, and an order in council was issued, requiring the directors of the Bank of England to suspend all payments in cash, until the sense of Parliament could be taken on the subject.

"The severe restrictions the bank attempted to place upon commerce, very greatly contributed to bring on the calamity by which it was subsequently overwhelmed. The issues, which were £14,000,000 when the exchange was against the country, were reduced to £8,640,250 when they had been for several months eminently favorable. It appears from the entire evidence in the reports, that it was the excessive restriction of notes which drained their vaults during the autumn of 1796, and that if they had been more liberal in their issues, their vaults would have been much better replenished with cash." *

"But while the price of public securities was great-

* Macleod, Theory and Practice of Banking, vol. ii, pp. 76–97.

ly affected, the effect of the contraction was hardly perceptible on the markets for goods. The price of corn had previously been falling from restored abundance, while from the opposite cause, scarcity, actual or apprehended, colonial produce continued to rise, notwithstanding not only the pressure on the money market, but notwithstanding, also, the advance of the exchanges. It is not possible to adduce an instance more striking of the inefficiency of a contraction of the circulation in counteracting the tendency to an advance of prices under the influence of actual scarcity, or of the force of opinion of prospective scarcity relatively to the estimated rate of consumption." *

The merchants, brokers, and shipowners of London met on the same day that the bank suspended specie payments, and resolved that they would continue to receive the notes of the bank in payment of all debts due them, and would make their own payments in them also. This had become necessary, in a measure, because the Government had only authorized the bank to cease the redemption of the notes in specie, but had not made them a legal tender. It was only in 1811, in the midst of the immense efforts made by England to overthrow Napoleon, and when Lord King threatened to force his tenants to pay their rents in gold or its equivalent, that the Government resorted to this extreme measure. The legal suspension lasted till 1822, but the bank in reality resumed cash payments in 1820, after which gold ceased to be at premium. The issues of the bank were carried as high as £29,500,000, principally in consequence of the necessities of the

* Tooke, History of Prices, vol. i, pp. 205, 206.

Government; and the premium on gold rose as high as 41 per cent. The suspension of the Bank of England gave rise to theories which yet control all legislation in regard to banks and bank issues, although all the facts upon which the theories are founded, when carefully analyzed and studied, refute them completely. Every rise of price produced by bad crops, and by the interruptions to commerce consequent upon war and non-intercourse between nations, were all attributed to a redundant currency. But to-day, thanks to the intelligence and industry of Mr. John Tooke, aided in his latter researches by Mr. Danson and Mr. Wm. Newmarch, all the fluctuations in prices during the suspension of the bank, as well as those since the resumption of cash payments in 1820, have been clearly traced to cost of production, and supply and demand—sole causes that affect prices, if there be any truth in political economy, which teaches that all the results of labor are controlled by natural laws, and not solely by man's actions or will. The following extracts from Mr. Tooke's "History of Prices" will greatly facilitate the comprehension of the question of paper money; but every one desirous of understanding the subject thoroughly, should read the whole of that able and interesting work.

| | |
|---|---|
| "The circulation of the Bank of England on August 31, 1794, was | £10,286,780 |
| The average circulation for the quarter ending September 30, 1794, | 10,422,900 |
| The average circulation for the quarter ending December 31, 1794 | 10,964,980 |
| The average circulation for the quarter ending March 31, 1795 | 12,421,260 |

"Notwithstanding these increased issues, the exchanges actually experienced some improvement". (*i. e.* became more favorable to England). (Vol. i, p. 198.)

"The circulation of the Bank, was

| | | | |
|---|---|---|---|
| On Feb. 28, 1795, | £14,017,510; | exchange on Hamburg | 36*s.* 0*d.* |
| Aug. 31, " | 10,862,200 | " " | 32*s.* 6*d.* |

Here was a decrease of 22½ per cent. in the circulation, accompanied by a rise of 10 per cent. in foreign exchange, the very reverse of the currency theory.

"At the close of 1795, a notice was exhibited at the doors of the bank, announcing that in future, only a certain proportion of the applications for discount would be complied with, however high might be the credit of the parties. This announcement, combined with the actual contraction of the issues, occasioned a very severe pressure on the money market, and in the spring of 1796 there were great complaints of an insufficiency of circulating medium for the trade in the metropolis." (Vol. i., p. 200.) The pressure in the money market here recorded is particularly deserving of notice, as showing that the high price of provisions in the spring of 1796, was not in any degree owing to an enlarged circulation. The circulation of the bank, exclusive of post bills, was:

| | | Average price of wheat in London market following 3 months. |
|---|---|---|
| On February 28, 1795, | £13,539,160; | 57*s.* per quarter. |
| " 1796, | 11,030,116; | 94*s.* " |

(Vol. I., p. 202.)

"The position of the bank was:

| | February 28, 1797. | August, 1798. |
|---|---|---|
| Circulation, | £9,674,780 | £12,180,610 |
| Deposits, | 4,891,530 | 8,300,720 |
| Securities, private, | 5,123,319 | 6,419,602 |
| Bullion, | 1,086,170 | 6,546,100 |

"This increased issue of paper was accompanied by a rise (fall*) of the exchanges, the rapid influx of bullion, and *a great fall in the prices of provisions.*" (Vol. i, pp. 206, 207.)

The real cause of the rise of gold was the demand for foreign payments. "Of the magnitude of the extra demand for immediate payments abroad, some idea may be formed by the fact that the foreign expenditures of the Government were

| | |
|---|---|
| In 1794 | £8,335,592 |
| 1795 | 11,040,236 |
| 1796 | 10,649,916 |
| Excess of naval stores imported in these years | 4,702,819 |
| Grain imported in these years | 7,44 ,012 |
| | £42,174,575 |

of which the largest proportion fell upon the last ten years." (Vol. i, p. 208.)

"If it was the amount of bank notes that raised prices in 1800 and 1801, how happened it that an increased amount in 1802 did not sustain the prices, and much more, prevent a fall of above 50 per cent.? And if the exchanges had been depressed (raised) and the price of bullion raised by the amount of the circulation, how happened it that they tended upon the abatement of foreign payments to their par level coincidently with increased issues, as will appear by the following statement:

| The average circulation | Exchange on Hamburg, Dec. 31. | For'n Gold. | Sil'r Dolls. | Wheat. |
|---|---|---|---|---|
| Of 1800 was £13,421,920 | 30*s.* 0*d.* | 4*l.* 6*s.* 0*d.* | 5*s.* 9*d.* | 133*s.* 0*d.* |
| 1801 " 13,454,370 | 31*s.* 11*d.* | 4*l.* 3*s.* 6*d.* | 5*s.* 10½*d.* | 75*s.* 6*d.* |
| 1802 " 13,917,980 | 34*s.* 0*d.* | 4*l.* 0*s.* 0*d.* | 5*s.* 4¼*d.* | 57*s.* 1*d.* |

(Vol. i, p. 249.)

* See note p. 115.

"The great rise of the prices of corn, and of other leading articles of consumption, some of them to a height beyond any which they ever afterward attained, and the great excitement in 1807 and 1809, *took place under a remarkably restricted and equable state of the bank circulation*, and in a state of the currency which, judging by the exchanges, and the price of bullion, and the position of the bank, as to its treasure, compared with its liabilities, was such as it might have been in a convertible state of the paper." (Vol. i, p. 291.)

"In the early part of 1809 there was a small increase of the amount of the bank circulation. Notwithstanding a further increase of bank notes, *the prices of nearly all commodities fell considerably with such increase.*" (Vol. i, p. 361.)

"But with these exceptions (lands, houses, and shipping), which, so explained, afford no ground for ascribing their comparatively high price to depreciation of money, nearly all other objects of exchange *were lower in price in* 1810 *and* 1811, *than in* 1800, *in few intances less than* 20 *per cent., and in some instances upward of* 50 *per cent., as measured in paper*, while gold had risen 25 per cent. (Vol. i, p. 313.)

"The discredit and distress in 1810 were clearly the consequence of the great fall of prices. Now if, as according to that theory is supposed, the rise of prices had been caused by an increase of Bank of England paper, how happened it, that with a further increased issue they should have fallen? And if that increased issue had not been enough, why should there not have been a still further issue, for the express purpose of supporting prices, and thus preventing the loss and discredit attending the fall?" (Vol. i, p. 357.)

"In 1810, the Bank of England increased its issues £4,500,000, and the exchanges rose (fell), that on Hamburgh from 28*s.* 4*d.* to 31*s.* 9*d.* and the price of gold fell from 4*l.* 11*s.* to 4*l.* 4*s.* 6*d.*" (Vol. i, p. 362.)

"Coincidently with the large discounts in 1810, the exchanges rose (fell), while the prices of commodities experienced a very considerable fall." (Vol. iii, p. 123.)

"In 1808, when the utmost extravagance of speculation prevailed, the amount of private securities held by the bank ranged at between 13 and 14 millions,—being no perceptible increase upon what it had been during the three or four years preceding. But the fall of prices thenceforward, was followed by a progressive increase of issues, through the medium of discounts, which in August, 1810, reached the enormous and unprecedented amount of £23,775,093. This greatly increased amount of discounts, and the consequent enlargement of the bank circulation, were coincident with the most depressed state of the markets, and with the greatest commercial distress. In proportion as markets and commercial credit tended to revival, the private securities held by the bank underwent a progressive diminution; and the amount in February, 1813,—a period which was precisely that in which the prices of both imported and exportable commodities, and of labor, were in the aggregate higher than in any former or subsequent period,—was reduced to £12,894,324, being a reduction of upward of 10 millions." (Vol. i, pp. 363–365.)

Mr. Hume says that at the very time that the bullionists in England were attributing every rise of price to overissues and depreciation of bank notes, "the prices of sugar and coffee, on the Continent, computed in gold, were four or five times higher than their prices in England, computed in bank notes. Coffee was worth in England, in bank notes, 6*d.* per pound, and on the Continent 3*s.* to 4*s.* Gold was worth in England, in bank notes, £5 per ounce, and on the Continent 3*l.* 17*s.* 10½*d.* in gold.

"It is too absurd, of course, to say literally and distinctly that the gold was remitted instead of the coffee, as a preferable mercantile operation; and yet if it was not so, under some explanation which I am totally unable to conjecture, what becomes of Mr. Huskisson's advice to the bank, to draw in a number of their notes, in order to reduce the price of coffee to the sum at which it would be a preferable remittance to gold. While gold was at a premium in England, there was not a place on the globe at which we could gain access with some goods, as a valuable consideration, from whence the gold and silver did not spontaneously flow to us; and there was not a country in the world in which so large a quantity of desirable goods could be obtained for an ounce of gold as in England. . . . It is a positive fact that England was the cheapest country in the world during the time when gold was 25 per cent. and upward above the mint price." * Yet Mr. Huskisson, in a speech delivered May 7th, 1811, asserted that it was a "fact admitted on all hands, that there was a profit of 20 per cent. made by the exportation of gold to France." †

* Tooke, History of Prices, vol. iii, pp. 107–109.

† Id., ib., vol. iii, p. 110.

| The circulation of £5 and upward was | | Price of wheat in December. |
|---|---|---|
| Last quarter of 1812, | £15,647,350. | 121 shillings. |
| " " 1813, | 16,092,590. | 73 " |
| " " 1814, | 18,502,690. | 65 " |
| In January, 1815, the price of wheat declined to | | 62 " |

(Vol. ii, p. 32.)

| Circulation of the Bank of England. | Price of Gold. | Ex. on Hamburg. | On Paris. |
|---|---|---|---|
| In Feb. 1814, £24,801,080. | 5*l*. 8*s*. | 29*s*. | frs. 21. |
| In Aug. " 28,368,290. | 4 5 | 33 | 23.30. |

(Vol. ii, pp. 28–30.)

The cause of this fall of gold and of the foreign exchanges was that the preliminaries of peace between France and the allies were signed in April, 1814.

"The landing of Napoleon in France in 1815, had the effect of instantly depressing (raising) the exchanges, and raising the price of gold in an extraordinary degree. The exchanges, which immediately previous to the intelligence of that event had been,

| | On Hamburg. | On Paris. | Price of Gold. |
|---|---|---|---|
| | 32.3. | frs. 22.10. | 4*l*. 9*s*. |
| Suddenly fell (rose) to | 28.0. | 18.80. | 5 7 |

"After the battle of Waterloo the exchanges rose (fell) and the price of gold fell as rapidly as they had just before tended in an opposite direction." (Vol. ii, p. 33.)*

* "On receipt of the news of Bonaparte's landing from Elba, the price of gold in the London market rose ten per cent. in one morning, and that without the slightest alteration whatever in the amount of the inconvertible issues of the bank. In the course of a few days more, the advance of price amounted to twenty per cent, and this advance was maintained until after the battle of Waterloo, when the price of gold fell nearly as rapidly as it had risen, and in a manner equally unaccounted for by any corresponding movement of the bank circulation. Than the rationale of these phenomena nothing can be simpler. A crisis had suddenly arisen which called for an instant and vast supply of gold, at whatever cost, for the

The rise of gold on this, and on every other occasion, could not have occurred were it not for the suspension of specie payments; for, with redemption of notes in specie, a drain of gold is invariably supplied at par from the bank vaults. Therefore a rise of gold above par is an impossibility as long as specie payments are maintained. But what would have been the condition of commercial affairs in 1815, had the bank then redeemed its notes in gold, and the bank act of 1844 been in existence? According to the theory of the advocates of "the currency principle" and of the bank act, every sovereign exported for the use of the armies would have required the withdrawal of an equal amount of bank notes from circulation; and, as the circulation can never be increased *beyond* the amount needed by the community, every decrease of the circulation consequent on the export of gold would have deprived the community of notes actually indispensable to the daily transactions, which would therefore have been diminished or arrested, to the great detriment of the entire community. This state of things is precisely what

equipment of armies, the remittance of subsidies, and the repletion of military chests. There was no time to wait till this supply could be brought from countries where there was gold in abundance; it must be procured on the spot, and that spot was one from which nearly all hoards of the precious metals had long been swept away. The price of gold, therefore, rose precisely on the same principle on which the price of corn rises in a famine; it rose to a famine rate, and again fell the moment the famine demand had ceased. And this great fact at once affords the most satisfactory demonstration of the futility of any scheme for testing the value of conventional notes by the price of gold, and furnishes the most unanswerable refutation of the theory which would ascribe all the variations of the price of gold during the continuance of the bank restrictions to the fluctuations of the bank issues." (Fullarton on the Regulation of Currencies, p. 23.)

heretofore has constantly occurred in the United States, from the erroneous action of the banks, every time that a temporary exportation of gold occurred.

"In 1817 gold was flowing in largely, and the bullion in the bank had, by August, reached the large amount—then without precedent—of £11,668,266. The circulation being then £29,503,000, nearly the highest amount attained by the outstanding notes of the Bank of England." (Vol. iii, page 131.)*

"According to what definition can it be contended that this rise in the price of coin, between the spring of 1816 and the summer of 1817, being coincident with an influx of upward of £7,000,000 of bullion into the coffers of the bank, raising the amount of it to a sum of £11,668,260—an amount beyond any that the bank had ever before possessed—should be considered as resulting from a depreciation of bank paper?" (Vol. ii, p. 18.)

"In short, turn the theory which ascribes the rise of coin in 1816 and 1817 to the local influence of our currency in every way possible, consistently with the facts, and it will be found to fail wholly and in all its parts." (Vol. ii, p. 19.)

"While the amount of the bank issues was, from 1797 to 1817, undergoing, with trifling exceptions, a progressive increase, *the exchanges, upon every pause*

* France offers a similar example of the precious metals flowing into a country while the issues of irredeemable paper currency were increasing. The Bank of France suspended specie payments on the 16th March, 1848, and resumed them on the 6th August, 1850. Its position was,

| | | | | | | |
|---|---|---|---|---|---|---|
| On the 6th April, 1848, | circulation, | frs. | 295,500,000; | bullion, | frs. | 97,000,000 |
| " 4th July, 1850, | " | " | 500,000,000 | " | " | 454,250,000† |

† Tooke, History of Prices, vol. vi, p. 61.

from the pressure of extraordinary foreign payments, tended to a recovery, and when this pressure had entirely ceased the exchanges and the price of gold were restored to par, while the bank circulation was larger in amount than at any preceding period." (Vol. i, pp. 157, 158.)

Fullarton says: "With only one or two exceptions, and those admitting of satisfactory explanation, every remarkable fall (rise) of the exchanges, followed by a drain of gold, that has occurred during the last half century, has been coincident throughout with a comparatively *low* state of the circulating medium, and *vice versa.* On no occasion was this proposition more strikingly exemplified than during the period immediately preceding the suspension of cash payments in 1797, when, for two years together, a system of the most determined contraction was carried on by the directors of the Bank of England with unrelenting perseverance, reducing the circulation from £16,017,510 on the 28th February, 1795, to £8,640,250 on the 25th February, 1797, without arresting, in the least apparent degree, the drain of gold which was then in progress for restoring the exchanges. The restoration of the exchanges to its bullion par, from a depression of full thirty per cent., was accomplished in 1816, after various remarkable vicissitudes, in the face of an enlargement of the issues of the Bank of England to an extent varying from three to six millions." *

The London Economist of 22d November, 1862, gives the following interesting table of the value of

* On the Regulation of Currencies, p. 120.

gold during the suspension of the bank, to which we annex the semiannual statements of the circulation:

| Average market price of Standard Gold, per oz. | | | | Average premium on Standard Gold. | | Circulation. February. | August. |
|---|---|---|---|---|---|---|---|
| 1809, | £4 | 10s. | 9d. | 16¼ | p. ct. | £18,542,860 | £19,574,180 |
| 1810, | 4 | 5 | 0 | 9 1/10 | " | 21,019,600 | 24,793,990 |
| 1811, | 4 | 17 | 1 | 24¼ | " | 23,360,220 | 23,286,850 |
| 1812, | 5 | 1 | 4 | 30 | " | 23,408,320 | 23,026,880 |
| Sept. to Dec. 1812, | 5 | 8 | 0 | 38¼ | " | | |
| 1813, | 5 | 6 | 2 | 36 1/10 | " | 23,214,930 | 24,828,120 |
| Nov. 1812, to March, 1813, | 5 | 10 | 0 | 41 | " | | |
| 1814, | 5 | 1 | 8 | 30¼ | " | 24,808,080 | 28,368,290 |
| 1815, | 4 | 12 | 9 | 18⅝ | " | 27,261,650 | 27,248,670 |
| 1816, | 4 | 0 | 0 | 2¼ | " | 27,013,620 | 26,758,720 |
| Oct. to Dec. 1816, | 3 | 18 | 6 | Less than 1 | " | | |
| 1817, | 4 | 0 | 0 | 2¼ | " | 27,397,900 | 29,543,780 |
| 1818, | 4 | 1 | 5 | 5¼ | " | 27,770,970 | 26,202,150 |
| 1819 to Feb. | 4 | 3 | 0 | 6¼ | " | 25 126,700 | 25,252,690 |
| 1820, | 3 | 17 | 10¼ | 0 | " | 23,484,110 | 24,299,340 |

The author of "Money," in the Encyclopædia Britannica, says: "The premium on gold in 1814 is an indigestible fact for those who contend that bank notes, being issued in proportion to the demand, have not been depreciated from excessive issues." But what evidence have we that the premium on gold in 1814 was the consequence of over issues of bank notes? We find gold in

| | | | | | |
|---|---|---|---|---|---|
| 1809, | at 16¼ | per ct. | premium, | with av'ge issues of | £19.000,000 |
| 1810, | " 9 1/10 | " | " | " " | 22.900,000 |
| 1811, | " 24¼ | " | " | " " | 23.300,000 |
| 1812, | " 30 | " | " | " " | 23,200,000 |
| 1813, | " 36 | " | " | " " | 24,000.000 |
| 1814, | " 30 | " | " | " " | 26,500,000 |
| 1815, | " 18⅝ | " | " | " " | 27,250.000 |
| 1816, | " 2¼ | " | " | " " | 26,900,000 |
| 1817, | " 2¼ | " | " | " " | 28.500.000 |
| 1818, | " 5¼ | " | " | " " | 27.000.000 |
| Feb. 1819, | " 6¼ | " | " | with issues of | 25,100,000 |
| 1820, | " Par | " | " | with av'ge issues of | 23,900,000 |

From 1809 to 1810, the circulation *increased* twenty

per cent., while the premium on gold *fell* seven per cent. From 1810 to 1811 the circulation increased less than two per cent., and yet the premium on gold rose fifteen and a half per cent. From 1811 to 1813 the circulation only increased three per cent., and yet the premium on gold increased eleven and a half per cent. From 1813 to 1814 the circulation *increased* ten per cent., while the premium on gold *fell* six per cent. From 1814 to 1815 the circulation *increased* nearly three per cent., while the premium on gold *fell* eleven per cent. From 1815 to 1816 the circulation decreased only a little over one per cent., and yet the premium on gold fell sixteen and a half per cent. From 1816 to 1817 the circulation increased five per cent., and yet the premium on gold remained the same as in 1816, whilst in 1818, with a *decrease* in the circulation of over five per cent., the premium on gold *more than doubled,* rising from two and a half to five and a half per cent. In 1819 the circulation *decreased* eight per cent., while the premium on gold *rose* one per cent. What connection can there be found here between the issues of bank notes and the premium on gold? And if the amount of the circulation had no influence on gold, how can it have influenced the prices of commodities and labor?

Mr. Tooke says: "The relatively high prices of articles divested of taxation, and not the objects of immediate war expenditure, in the interval from 1793 to 1814, may be ascribed to the following general circumstances:

"1. The frequent recurrence of seasons of an unfavorable character, there having been in that interval no fewer than eleven seasons (1794, 1795, 1798, 1800,

1804, 1807 to 1812) in which the general produce of corn, but more especially of wheat, was deficient.

"2. The destruction of a great source of supply of transatlantic produce by the revolution in St. Domingo, which rendered sugar and coffee, and most other West India produce, scarce and dear during the earlier part of the war.

"3. Obstructions and prohibitions of export from the Continent of Europe of articles of which, whether as raw materials of our manufactures, or naval stores, or food, we stood in urgent need.

"4. The increased cost of importation, by higher freights and insurance, incidental to a state of war generally, aggravated by the peculiar commercial hostility and exclusion which marked the latter years.

"5. The difference of exchange, which in the last five years of the war averaged twenty per cent.*

"6. A higher rate of interest, in consequence of the absorption, by the war loans, of a considerable proportion of the savings of individuals."

"The causes of the decline, and of the lower range of prices, from 1814 to 1837, except 1816–'17, which was a moment of great scarcity over all Europe, were:

"1. A succession of more favorable seasons, in the last twenty years from 1818, there having been but five seasons in which the produce of wheat was decidedly deficient.

"2. The removal of obstacles from the several sources of foreign supply; a great extension of some of them, and the discovery of new ones.

* Tooke estimates the extra war charges of freight, insurance, and loss on exchange on wheat, at 44*s.* per quarter! (Vol. ii, p. 207.)

"3. A great reduction of the charges of importation, by low freights and insurances, and the improved and cheaper and more rapid internal communication.

"4. A rise (fall) in the foreign exchanges, and consequent reduction of the cost of all imported commodities.

"5. Improvements in machinery, in chemistry, and in the arts and sciences generally, all tending to reduce the cost of production of numerous articles, or to provide cheaper substitutes.

"6. A reduction of the rate of interest."*

"There is not, as far as I have been able to discover, any single commodity in the whole range of articles embraced in the most extensive list of prices, the variations of which do not admit of being distinctly accounted for by circumstances peculiar to it, in the relation of supply, actual or contingent, real or apprehended, to the ordinary rate of consumption, without supposing any influence from the bank restriction *beyond the degree in which the difference of exchange, which could not have existed but for the restriction*,† may be considered to have operated distinctly on the cost of production."‡

"McCulloch states 'that there is not a single commodity that has fallen in price since 1814, the fall of which may not be satisfactorily accounted for without reference to the supply of gold and silver.' It seems to

* History of Prices, vol. ii, pp. 346, 348.

† The words we have italicised prove how unfounded is the criticism of Mr. Macleod when he says: "We can hardly think Mr. Tooke can be correct in so *entirely excluding the effect of the depreciation of the paper currency as he does*" (Theory and Practice of Banking, vol. ii, p. 179.)

‡ History of Prices, vol. ii, p. 349.

follow that the previous rise may be equally accounted for without such reference." *

"At the end of 1824 and beginning of 1825 the spirit of speculation in articles of consumption had amounted to positive infection, numbers of persons being induced to go out of their own line of business to speculate in articles with which they had no concern whatever, but induced by representations of their brokers to do so in the hope of realizing great and immediate gains. The recognition of the independence of the South American States and Mexico, opened out at this period a boundless field for speculation and the consumption of British manufactures, and the spirit of speculation was aggravated to the utmost by the visions of countless wealth which was to be extracted from the gold and silver producing countries, and immense schemes were formed for working the mines with British capital. Besides which, when the juvenile republics wanted to borrow money to support their public credit, the British capitalists were only too eager to lend it. It is alleged that £150,000,000 of British capital was sunk in different ways in Mexico and South America."

"The speculative fever was at its height in the first four months of 1825; after May and June the decline was rapid. The South American loans and the Mexican mining schemes proved almost universally total losses. Universal discredit now succeeded, goods became unsalable, so that stocks, which are usually held in anticipation of demand, were wholly unavailable to meet the pecuniary engagements of the holders. In

* Tooke, History of Prices, vol. ii, p. 353.

May the Bank of England endeavored violently to contract its issues. The bullion, which stood above £14,000,000 in January, 1824, was reduced to £11,600,000 in October, 1824, and yet the bank had increased its issues £2,300,000. In April, 1825, the bullion was further diminished by upward of £4,000,000, and their issues were £3,600,000 higher when they had only £6,650,000 of bullion than when they had £14,000,000."

"On the 29th November, 1825, it was announced that Sir William Elford's—a large bank at Plymouth—had failed, and that was immediately followed by the fall of Wentworth & Co., a great Yorkshire firm. By the 3d December, the panic had fairly set in, and the whole city was thrown into the most violent state of alarm and consternation. On that day, Saturday, some of the directors were informed that the house of Pole, Thornton & Co., one of the leading city banking houses, was in difficulties, and at a hurried meeting held on the following day, it was decided to place £300,000 at their disposal upon proper security. During the week the house sustained itself, but the storm, instead of abating, became more furious than ever, and on Monday, 18th December, Pole & Co. finally stopped payment. The fall of this great banking house was the signal for a general run upon all the London bankers, and three or four more gave way, and spread universal consternation among the country banks, sixty-three of which succumbed to the crisis, though a considerable number paid 20*s*. in the pound, and eventually resumed business. From Monday, the 12th, to Saturday, the 17th December, was the height of the crisis in London."

"On the day after Pole & Co. fell, another house of

equal magnitude fell, Williams, Burgess & Co. The panic then became universal, and as the directors of the Bank of England thought that they would certainly have to stop payment, they sounded the Government as to a restriction act, but the Government absolutely declined it, and it was resolved that the bank should pay away its last sovereign. On the Saturday the coin in bank vaults scarcely exceeded one million, but when the Saturday evening came the tide receded, and the directors were able to assure the ministry that all danger was over. On Monday, the 19th, about £400,000 came from France, and the demands having sensibly abated, the supplies from the mint fully equalled or rather exceeded the sums drawn from the bank."

"Mr. Huskisson said afterward in the House of Commons, that during forty eight hours (Monday and Tuesday, December 12th and 13th) it was impossible to convert into money, to any extent, the best securities of the Government. Persons could neither sell exchequer bills, nor bank stock, nor East India stock, nor the public funds. Mr. Baring said that men would not part with their money on any terms, nor for any security. The extent to which the distress had reached was melancholy to the last degree. Persons of undoubted wealth and real capital did not know whether they should be able to meet their engagements for the next day. By this time, however, the exchanges had decidedly turned in favor of the country, and on Wednesday, the 14th, the bank totally changed their policy, and discounted with the utmost profuseness. They made enormous advances on exchequer bills, and securities of all sorts. This audacious policy was crowned with the most complete success; the panic was stayed almost immediately. Between Wednesday, the 14th, and Saturday, the 17th, the bank issued upward of £5,-000,000 of notes. By the 24th December, the panic was completely allayed all over the country, and the amount of the one-pound notes the bank issued was under £500,000, and by the beginning of 1826 the credit of the banking world was completely restored. Had the bank on Monday, the 12th, adopted the course which was adopted on Wednesday, the 14th, the whole of that terrific crisis would have been avoided. Sir Peter Pole & Co. had a surplus of £170,000 after payment of all claims against them, besides large landed property belonging to Sir Peter Pole, and about £100,-000, the private property of other members of the firm. Williams, Burgess & Co. had enough to pay 40*s.* in the pound."

"When the causes of this terrible calamity came to be discussed, there were not wanting many who laid the whole blame upon the excessive issues of the bank, as well as the excessive issues of the country banks. But though it is indisputable that the bank acted on the most unsound principles, in not contracting its issues when the great drain of bullion for exportation was going on, it is a mere delusion for men to attribute the consequences of their own wild and extravagant mania to the Bank of England, or to any bank. The errors of all the banks put together were trivial compared to the outbreaks of speculative insanity which seized upon all classes. It was not the issue of some bank notes more or less which originated the calamity, but the insatiable thirst for growing suddenly rich, that seized upon so many persons, and led them to embark in the maddest schemes, totally out of their line of business. Was it the issue of bank notes that led a respectable bookselling firm to risk £100,000 on a speculation in hops?" *

Immediately after the ministry refused their assent to the application of the bank for authority to suspend specie payments, a conference was held between Lord Liverpool, the Prime Minister, Mr. Huskisson, the Chancellor of the Exchequer, the Governor of the Bank, and Mr. Baring, afterward Lord Ashburton. At this conference it was resolved to resort to the right of the bank to issue one-pound notes granted in 1797, but which had not been exercised for some time. A box containing 600,000 or 700,000 of these one-pound notes, which had been put aside unused, had been discovered by accident; they were immediately issued in the week ending 24th December, 1825, and relieved the bank of a demand for gold to that extent, as these bank notes, to the country bankers, were as good as sovereigns. This accidental discovery and issue of one-pound notes, is generally acknowledged to have saved the bank from suspension and the country from the injurious consequences that would have followed, and yet Parliament, at its next session, passed an act prohibiting all issues of notes under £5 after 1829! †

* Macleod, Theory and Practice of Banking, vol. ii, pp. 241–254.

† "The limitation to £5 in England is a disgrace to monetary science and commercial practice among us. We have never heard one decently plausible reason assigned for it. It had its origin in the alarm created by the frequent insolvency of banks of issue, and in an ignorance of currency, which threw away the only advantage for which a paper currency was invented. Paper was designed to supersede gold, in order to escape the ex-

The issues of the bank were, in the week ending

| | |
|---|---|
| Dec. 3, 1825 | £17,477,298 |
| " 10, " | 18,037,960 |
| " 17, " | 23,942,810 |
| " 24, " | 25,611,800 |
| " 31, " | 25,709,410 |
| Feb. 28, 1826 | 25,467,910* |

This expansion of the bank, and its effects, fully sustained the views taken by the celebrated Bullion Committee of the House of Commons in 1810, who stated that it was the duty of the Bank of England to sustain credit by expanding its issues in moments of panic.

"The highest average circulation of the bank in the quarter ending 31st of March, 1825, when the speculative mania was at its height, was £21,084,470; that of the quarter ending 31st of August, 1826, was £21,563,560, and the bullion £6,784,230; and the quarter ending 28th of February, 1827, was £21,890,610, and the bullion £10,159,020. Thus, with a circulation larger than it had been at its highest period in 1825 (with the exception of the last three weeks in December), there was in little more than twelve months from the nearly complete exhaustion of the coffers of the bank in December, 1825, such a state of the exchanges as raised the treasure to upward of 10 millions." †

pense of the metal; and obviously convenience and safety of payment ought alone to restrict the use of paper. The theorists who talked of excessive issues, naturally set their faces against one-pound notes; but not one of them has ever been able to tell the world why the Bank of England should not circulate its promises to pay one pound on demand among those who trust it, or why a banker who is unsafe for issuing one-pound notes, is not unsafe also for issuing fives." ("What is Money?" North British Review, November, 1861.)

* Tooke, History of Prices, vol. ii, p. 188.

† Id., ib., p. 189.

In 1844 was passed the celebrated Bank Act of Sir Robert Peel. Mr. Tooke calls it "the unwise and mischievous act of 1844." * It divided the bank into two distinct departments, the banking and the issue departments. Disregarding the important fact that circulation should vary with the variations in the operations of the community, the bill limited the issues of the bank to £14,000,000, being about the amount of the loans of the bank to the state.† Sir Robert Peel had become convinced that the circulation of the bank could not be reduced below £14,000,000, and he therefore adopted that amount as the maximum issues of notes against securities. For all issues beyond that amount, the issue department was to receive and hold gold, either sovereigns or bullion, to an equivalent amount, the idea being that for every bank note issued beyond that amount, a similar amount of gold should be withdrawn from the circulation, so as to permit the latter to be further expanded by nothing but gold. "All existing banks of issue were to be at liberty to continue to issue an amount not exceeding the average of their issues during the twelve weeks next preceding the 27th of April, 1844. If two or more banks become united, the united bank may issue notes to the aggregate amount of the issues of each separate bank. If any banker who on the 6th of May, 1844, was issuing his own notes, should cease to do so, it is lawful for the crown in council to authorize the bank to increase its issues to any amount not exceeding two thirds of the amount of notes

* History of Prices, vol. iii, p. 114.

† The circulation of the bank in 1844 was £14,475,000, and its capital £14,553,000.

withdrawn from circulation:* all profits from the issues above £14,000,000 to go to the state. The avowed object of the act of 1844 was to take the regulation of the currency out of the hands or even the power of the directors of the Bank of England. The authors of the act of 1844 flattered themselves that for every five sovereigns that left the country, a five-pound note must be withdrawn from circulation." † "Sir Robert Peel deliberately took away the power of the bank to act in extreme occasions, under the impression that his act would prevent these extreme occasions from occurring." ‡ The object of the bill was thus stated at the time by Mr. S. J. Lloyd (afterward Lord Overstone), the great advocate of the measure, whose views had been adopted by Sir Robert Peel and incorporated in the bill: "contraction of circulation is to be made precisely coincident, as regards both time and amount, with diminution of the bullion; and thus it is conceived that the danger of total exhaustion, which could not befall a metallic circulation, will be rendered equally impossible with respect to a mixed circulation of gold and paper." § In

* "There is no reason which can be alleged for insisting on the substitution of gold or of Bank of England notes secured on a deposit of gold, for one third of the country circulation displaced (he should have said discontinued), which might not with equal force be urged for discarding the entire credit currency of the country and replacing it with a circulation of the metals." (Fullarton on the Regulation of Currencies, p. 193.)

† Macleod, Theory and Practice of Banking, vol. ii, pp. 300–303.

‡ Id., ib., p. 299.

§ Tooke, History of Prices, vol. iii, p. 282.

"Col. Torrens, in 'An Inquiry,' &c., in 1844, said: 'The proposed system will effectually prevent the recurrence of those cycles of commercial excitement and depression of which our ill-regulated currency has been the primary and exciting cause. When the Government plan shall have been

other words, the issues of bank notes in England were to be, thereafter, governed by the celebrated "currency principle," which "shortly stated is this—that when bank notes are permitted to be issued, the number in circulation should always be exactly equal to the coin which would be in circulation if they did not exist. The advocates of this principle maintain that it is the only true mode of regulating a paper currency, and preserving the paper of equal value with the gold coin." *

carried into effect, the abstraction of £7,000,000 of treasure from the coffers of the bank, in a period of nine months, will be morally impossible. Had the system existed in 1838 and 1839, it would have been utterly impossible that the drain should have extended to £7,000,000.' The following figures from the actual returns of the bank under the act, afford a striking illustration of the correctness of these views:

| | | | | | |
|---|---|---|---|---|---|
| 12th September, | 1846, | bullion, | £16,350,000; | circulation, | £20,920,000 |
| 24th April, | 1847, | " | 9,210,000 | " | 20,690,000 |
| | Decrease, | | 7,140,000 | | 230,000" |

(Tooke, History of Prices, vol. iii, p. 283.)

* Mr. James Wilson says: "These principles (the currency principles), and the course pursued by Sir Robert Peel, necessarily involve the following five assumptions:

"First. That the bank notes, though payable in coin, at the option of the holder, are still liable to be issued in excess, and are consequently subject to depreciation.

"Second. That convertibility is not alone a sufficient guarantee that a mixed currency of bank notes and coin shall conform in its variations to the same laws that would regulate a purely metallic currency.

"Third. That issuers of bank notes have power to increase or decrease the circulation at pleasure.

"Fourth. That by an expansion or contraction of the issues of bank notes at pleasure, the prices of commodities can be increased or diminished; and,

"Fifth. That by such increase or diminution of prices, the foreign exchanges will be corrected, and an undue influx or efflux of bullion, as the case may be, will be arrested." (Id., ib., p. 261.)

The advocates of the currency principles "consider that a purely metallic circulation (excepting only as regards the convenience and economy of

That is to say, the only proper issues of bank notes are those which represent an equivalent amount of coin in the hands of the issuers, with which to redeem the notes issued, like those of the Banks of Amsterdam and Hamburg. According to these views, bank notes being more convenient than coin for large commercial operations, it is proper and advantageous to withdraw coin and substitute in its place an equivalent amount of bank notes. But to use bank notes instead of coin, as counters representing commodities and services, is

paper) is the type of a perfect currency, and contend that the only sound principle of a mixed currency is that by which the bank notes in circulation should be made to conform to the gold into which they are convertible, not only in value, but in amount; that is to say, that the bank notes, being a substitute, and the only substitute, for so much coin, should vary exactly in amount as the coin would have done if the currency had been purely metallic." (Tooke, History of Prices, vol. iii, pp. 167, 168.)

"The propounders of the theory of the currency principle assume and affirm that it is in the power of the banks to act directly on their circulation; in other words, that they *can* and *do* exercise a direct control over the quantity of paper currency which they define to be bank notes." (Id., ib., p. 171.)

"According to the currency principle, the golden rule to be observed in the management of the circulation is—that in conformity to the assumed analogy of a metallic currency, a contraction should take place immediately on the commencement of a drain, and be continued, *pari passu* with the progress of the drain, until the drain and the consequent contraction of the circulation should so have reduced prices as through their medium to have turned the foreign exchanges—to have stopped the further export of gold—and to have superinduced an influx of it." (Id., ib., vol. v, p. 589.)

"But this doctrine (that contraction will prevent exports of bullion) is built upon two fallacies: first, that prices are governed by the expansions and contractions of the bank-note circulation; and, secondly, that a moderate reduction of prices is all that is necessary to create a market for your commodities in foreign countries." (Fullarton on the Regulation of Currencies, p. 130.)

injurious and improper. The foundation of this idea is the supposition that all bank notes are ultimately redeemed in coin, whereas they are almost all redeemed by being paid in, in payment of the loans which led to their issue. *

The act of 1844 is based on several capital errors. Upon what plea should the issue be separated from the banking department? † Why should not the supply

* "The mode of issue of bank notes is invariably through the medium of loans and discounts. . . . The reflux (of the bank notes) takes place chiefly in two ways: by payment of the redundant amount to a banker on a deposit account, or by the return of notes in discharge of securities on which advances have been made. A third way is, that of a return of the notes to the issuing bank by a demand for coin. The last seems, in the views of the currency theory, to be the only way by which a redundancy, arising from the unlimited power of issue, which they assume to exist, admits of being corrected in a convertible state of the paper. It is certainly the one least in use." (Tooke, History of Prices, vol. iii, p. 185.)

† "The issue department *is acted upon by the public*, while the banking department *acts upon the public*, thus producing a result the very reverse of that contemplated by the propounders of the scheme of separation. If then the due regulation of the currency depends, as it undoubtedly does, upon the banking department, and not upon the issue department, it is the height of inconsistency to restrict the latter and to leave the former entirely at the discretion of the directors." (Id., ib., vol. v, pp. 546, 547.)

"The union of functions, instead of being incongruous and incompatible, as—most gratuitously, without authority or proof from experience or reasoning—they are held to be by the currency school, would, in truth, be eminently conducive to congruity of interests, and harmony or perfect compatibility of action. Supposing that two large banking establishments had originally been formed in a separate state, the one similar to the present issue department, the other to the banking department, a correct view to the respective interests of the proprietors, and to the convenience of the public, would have led to the proposal of an amalgamation." (Id., ib., vol. v, pp. 553, 554.)

"Mr. George Carr Glyn, in his evidence before the committee of the House of Lords in 1848, said he had been of opinion, before the act

of currency be in proportion to the demand? If issues beyond £14,000,000 be injurious, why not also those under that amount? Are state stocks proper reserves with which to redeem bank notes payable in coin, on demand? * If a bank attempt to realize state stocks in a moment of embarrassment, when its notes are being presented for redemption in coin, can their realization fail to depreciate sensibly the value of the state stocks and thus aggravate existing difficulties? It must not be forgotten that the main difficulty in moments of commercial crisis, is that confidence is shaken; most holders of commodities and securities become eager sellers; purchasers are not to be found, and consequently property cannot be realized, and thus becomes useless as means of meeting pressing liabilities. Had Sir Robert Peel's act been in operation in 1825, the bank would, inevitably, have had to suspend specie payments. That calamity was then averted, not by restricting, but by augmenting the issues of the bank. It is evident that issues of paper money should be diminished when money is abundant and interest low, and augmented when money is scarce and in demand and interest high. The Bank Act of 1844 entirely disregards this, and forces the bank to act on the opposite theory. Mr. Tooke, Mr. Hawes, M. P., Mr. Hastie, M. P., Lord Ashburton, Mr. John Stuart Mill, Mr. Fullarton, and Mr. James Wilson, editor of the London Economist, all predicted the failure

passed, that the division of the bank into the issue and banking department was a desirable experiment; but after the experience of the preceding year, he considered that it had decidedly failed." (Macleod, Theory and Practice of Banking, vol. ii, p. 325.)

* "The issuing of notes upon the public funds is the most vicious principle possible." (Id., ib., p. 302.)

of the act of 1844, and that instead of preventing crises and panics, it would aggravate them. Tooke said, "The theory sought to be explained and established as forming the grounds for the measure of 1844, is in every point of view erroneous, proceeding, as it does, on an ambiguous use of language, on unfounded assumptions of principles and facts, and on false analogies." *

"In August, 1846, the bullion in the bank amounted to £16,366,000 with discount at 3 per cent. The crops of 1846 proved to be bad, and it became certain that an immense quantity of bullion would require to be exported in payment of the grain it would be necessary to import. Accordingly, from the middle of September, 1846, a steady and continuous drain of bullion set in, but the bank made no alteration in the rate of discount until the 16th of January, 1847, when the bullion having fallen to £13,949,000, it raised the discount to 3½; and on the 23d, the bullion having been further diminished £500,000, it raised the rate to 4 per cent. The drain still continued, but the bank made no further advance in the rate till the 10th of April, when its treasure being reduced to £9,867,000, it raised the rate of discount to 5 per cent. By the division of the bank into two distinct departments, the public saw that the whole banking resources of the bank were reduced to £2,558,000, and a complete panic seized both the public and the directors. The latter adopted measures of the most unprecedented severity to check the demand for notes. Merchants who had received loans were called upon to repay them without being permitted to renew them. During some days it was impossible to get bills

* History of Prices, vol. iii, p. 260.

discounted at all. The rate of discount for the best bills rose to 9, 10, and 12 per cent. During all this time *the price of wheat continued steadily to rise, notwithstanding the monetary pressure.*"

"The pressure passed off after the first week in May, having lasted about three weeks, and bullion began to flow in after the 24th April, until, at the end of June, it amounted to £10,526,000."

"The enormous importations of breadstuffs in May, June, and July, coupled with the very favorable appearance of the harvest, caused a heavy and continuous fall in the price of grain; the price of wheat, which, at the close of May, had been as high as 131*s.*, fell to 49*s.* 6*d.* in September. This was attended with ruin to the houses which had speculated in corn. The failures in the corn trade began in August, the miminum rate of discount was raised to 5½, and the greater part of the paper discounted was charged at much higher rates, even up to 7 per cent."

"On the 9th August the first of the frightful catalogue of failures began. Leslie, Alexander & Co. stopped payment with liabilities amounting to £500,000. In three weeks the failures were £3,027,000. Week after week followed, each one increasing in severity, until at last the total failures exceeded £15,000,000. Almost all the firms connected with the Mauritius failed, principally from having their funds locked up in sugar plantations. This was accompanied by immense failures in the India trade. The railway works which had been sanctioned in the session of 1845-'6, were now in full course of construction, causing an immense demand for ready money. Almost every tradesman in the kingdom was deep in railway speculations. Ever since the 26th June, the diminution of bullion had been going on rapidly. On the 2d October it was reduced to £8,565,-000, and the reserve to £3,409,000. The extreme pressure may be considered to have begun on the 23d September, when the bank adopted more stringent measures for curtailing the demand upon its resources. On the 2d October the bank gave notice that the minimum rate on all bills falling due before the 15th October, would be 5½ per cent.; and it refused altogether to make advances on stock or exchequer bills. This last announcement created a great excitement on the stock exchange. The town and country bankers hastened to sell their public securities to convert them into money. The difference between the price of consols for ready money, and that for the account of the 14th October, showed a rate of interest equivalent to 50 per cent. per annum. On the 16th October the bank rates of discount varied from 5½ to 9 per cent. At this time the bullion was £8,431,000; the reserve £2,-630,000. The following week, from Monday, the 18th, to Saturday, the 23d, was the great crisis. On that Monday, the Royal Bank of Liverpool, with a paid-up capital of £800,000, stopped payment, which caused the funds to fall 2 per cent. This was followed by the stoppage of the North and South Wales Bank, the Liverpool Banking Co., the Union Bank of Newcastle, heavy runs on the other banks in the district, and other bank failures at Manchester and in the west of England. A complete cessation of private discounts followed. No one would part with the money or notes in his possession."

"The continued and ever-increasing severity of the crisis caused deputation after deputation to be sent to the Government, to obtain a relaxation of the act, and on Saturday, the 23d October, the final determination of the ministry to authorize the bank to issue notes beyond the limits prescribed by the act, was taken, and communicated to the bank, who immediately acted upon it, and discounted freely at 9 per cent. The letter itself (authorizing the bank to issue notes beyond the limit of the act) was not actually sent till Monday, the 25th. No sooner was this letter made public, than the panic vanished like a dream ! Mr. Gurney stated that it produced its effects in ten minutes ! No sooner was it known that notes *might* be had, than the want of them ceased ! Not only did no infringement of the act take place, but the whole issue of notes in consequence of this letter was only £400,000 ; so that while at one moment the whole credit of Great Britain was in imminent danger of total destruction, within one hour it was saved by the issue of £400,000.*

* Macleod, Theory and Practice of Banking, vol. ii, pp. 306–314.

"Nothing could shake the steady resolve of the Government to maintain the restrictions of the act of 1844, until the London bankers had a meeting on Friday, 22d October, at which it was agreed that, if Government would not sanction a deviation from the act on the part of the bank, they would withdraw their whole balances from it. This was decisive. The bankers' balances in the Bank of England were £1,774,472, and the reserve in the bank to meet this amount was only £1,600,025. The bankers' resolution was communicated to Government on Saturday, the 23d, and early on Monday, the 25th, the celebrated letter, signed by Lord John Russell and the Chanceller of the Exchequer was sent to the bank, authorizing a deviation from the act. The bank was authorized to issue notes beyond the limit prescribed by the act, at a rate of discount fixed at eight per cent." (Alison's History of Europe, vol. viii, p. 109, American edition.)

Mr. Hubbard, Governor of the Bank of England, said on his examina-

"Thus did the famous Bank Charter Act, after having been three years in unrestrained operation, break down from the effect of its own provisions, but not until it had brought the country to the very verge of ruin. Three months after Lord John Russell's letter was written, the rate of discount was lowered to 4 per cent., a decisive proof that the previous high rates had been entirely owing to a want of *currency*, and not of *capital*."

"The common opinion is, that if there is an over issue of bank notes, it will drive the gold out of the country. That was the fundamental position of the famous bullion report in 1811, and it has been the basis of all our subsequent legislation on the subject. But in this case the very reverse took place; for when it was known that notes would be freely issued, *hoards* of gold immediately made their appearance, and the stock of bullion in the bank instantly began to increase."

"The effect of the infraction of the law, according to the Chancellor of the Exchequer's statement, was altogether magical; the whole panic ceased; the notes came out, the gold came in, all at the same time, and confidence was at last restored, all in consequence of the announced violation of the Bank Act. Apparently, that is an act honored more in the breach than the observance; but what is to be said in defence of an act which never proves beneficial till it is repealed?" *

"The crisis of 1847 was unlike any other that had

tion before a committee of the House of Commons in 1848: "The limitation of paper issues is the very essence of the act of 1844. *And as limitation operates sensibly only under circumstances of pressure*, it is obvious that to evade its stringency because a pressure is felt, is simply to stultify the act."

* Bankers' Magazine, New York, January, 1863, p. 537.

ever occurred, and well illustrated the working of the new law on the subject. There was no overtrading; there was no commercial embarrassment irrespective of the monetary pressure; the credit of the Bank of England was above suspicion; there was no run upon the other banks; capital was abundant and more than equal, as the events of the following years demonstrated, to all the undertakings which were in hand or in contemplation. There was simply and only a want of currency to make the advances with, because the bank, restrained by the act of 1844, could not lend money with a few hundred thousand pounds only in the banking department, though, in the other end, they had above £8,000,000 in the issue department." *

Sir Robert Peel himself said, in the parliamentary debates of 1848: "The bill of 1844 had a triple object. *Its first object was that in which I admit it has failed,* namely, to prevent, by early and gradual, severe and sudden contraction, and the panic and confusion inseparable from it." †

* Alison's History of Europe, vol. viii, chap. xliii, p. 100, American edition.

"With upward of £16,000,000 bullion in hand, the bank, when called upon to meet a drain for foreign payment, the actual extent of which did not reach nearly half that amount, and which, in all probability, would not, under the least vigilant management conceivable, have reached £10,000,000, found itself so crippled by the arbitrary separation of its departments, that the directors were under the necessity of resorting to measures more severely restrictive of commercial credit than any that had been known since 1796–'7." (Tooke, History of Prices, vol. iii, pp. 399, 400.)

† Macleod, Theory and Practice of Banking, vol. ii, p. 320.

Lord Ashburton said, in 1848, in his Financial or Commercial Crisis Considered: "The expectations entertained of this infallible panacea (the act of 1844) were unfounded—it would only work in fair weather, when restrictions of all sorts are inoperative and immaterial—it could not fail to break

He insisted, however, that it had greatly contributed to maintain the convertibility of the bank notes into specie. But the able author of the article "What is Money?" in the North British Review, November, 1861, says very well: "The loud preaching on the necessity of protecting the convertibility of the paper currency, which ushered in the act of 1844, was absurd; it was a cry for medicine for a healthy man. No one ever felt uneasy about the payment of the notes; but many trembled at the peril of not obtaining discount for their bills."

Tooke closes his review of the Bank Act of 1844 and of the crisis of 1847 as follows: * "As the result of a

down under the first difficulty—and it is in fact a serious aggravation, if not indeed the actual cause of the distress we now experience."

"Now this fright of the bank, with ten millions in her coffers, of violating this parliamentary restraint, has driven her into proceedings which have depreciated, to a very great extent, every description of property, food only, for evident reasons, excepted. It must not be easy to estimate this depreciation, extending over all merchandise, stocks, railroad shares, &c.; it probably would not have been overstated at from ten to twenty per cent. But what is worse, it has paralyzed this property in the hands of the possessors, rendered it unavailable toward meeting their engagements, and thus produced, in many cases, pecuniary sacrifices, much beyond the mere depreciation of the value of the property itself. It has further occasioned the suspension of the execution of orders from our customers in every quarter, thus distressing manufacturers, and impeding those very operations which would have corrected the tendency to an unfavorable balance of trade, and given safety to the circulation of the bank." (Tooke, History of Prices, vol. iii, p. 306.)

John Horsley Palmer, Esq., and Samuel Gurney, Esq., testified, in 1848, before a committee of the House of Commons, that the crisis of 1847 was, in their opinion, entirely caused by the restrictions of the act of 1844. Charles Turner, Esq., of Liverpool, testified before the same committee, that in his opinion, had the act not been suspended, universal bankruptcy would have been the issue.

* History of Prices, vol. iii, pp. 401, 402.

"The whole scheme (Bank Act of 1844) in truth is built upon assump-

careful examination of the principle on which the act of 1844 was founded, and of the experience of its working since the time when it came into operation, I have no hesitation in giving it as my opinion that it is a total, unmitigated, uncompensated, and, in its consequences, a lamentable failure." And he recommends "a total abrogation of those provisions of the acts of 1844 and 18₋5 which limit the amount of the note circulation and separate the function of issue from that of banking in the business of the Bank of England."

The rapid and injudicious contraction of the discounts of the New York city banks in September and October 1857, produced a financial crisis in the United States which reacted with great severity on Europe. "At the commencement of the year, the aspect of monetary affairs seemed to promise a long period of commercial ease. But subsequently, the outbreak of the mutiny in India, the consequent suspension of remittances from that quarter, and the inverse demand for specie, and a constant efflux of the precious metals from other causes; the demand for capital to supply the military materials to the Government and the East India Company; all these causes produced a depressing effect on the funds. In August consols fell to 90, being lower than at any time since January, 1856, during the pressure of the Russian war."

"Early in October monetary disaster loomed in the distance. The American mails brought tidings of the stoppage of banks of high standing and vast circulation, and of the failure of mercantile houses. On the receipt

tions which will not bear the test of examination." (Fullarton on the Regulation of Currencies, p. 113.)

of these evil tidings, the Bank of England raised the rate of discount from 5½ to 6 per cent.; on the 12th of October, it further raised it to 7 per cent., on the 19th to 8 per cent. On the 27th of October, a great shock to public credit and a consequent demand on the Bank of England for discounts arose from the failure of the Liverpool Borough Bank, (*not a bank of issue,*) with liabilities to the extent of £5,000,000, and whose re-discounted bills were largely held by the bill brokers and others in London. On the 4th of November, the rate of discount was further advanced by the bank to 9 per cent.—an unprecedented rate, for when the bank act was suspended in 1847, the then rate, which was also the rate stipulated by the Government, was 8 per cent. The bullion, which was on the 10th of October £10,110,000, was now only £7,919,000. By this time, however, the Continental drain for gold had ceased, the American demand had become unimportant, and there was little apprehension that the bank issues would be inadequate to meet the necessities of commerce, within the legalized sphere of their circulation."

"Upon this state of things supervened, on the 7th of November, the failure of Dennistoun & Co., with liabilities of £2,000 000, and on the 9th, that of the Western Bank of Glasgow, with liabilities between 6 and 7 millions, when the rate of discount was advanced by the bank to 10 per cent.! On the 11th, was received the news of the failure of the City of Glasgow Bank, with liabilities of £6,000,000, which was followed by the suspension of the large discount firm of Sanderson Sandiman & Co., of London, for £5,500,000. All this, and a renewed discredit in Ireland, caused the abstraction from the bank vaults, in four weeks, of upward of two millions of gold to supply the wants of Scotland and Ireland; of which amount more than one million was sent to Scotland and £280,000 to Ireland between the 5th and 12th of November. This drain was in its nature sudden and irresistible, and acted necessarily on the reserve, which on the 11th of November had decreased to £1,462,000 and the bullion to £6,666,000. The public had become alarmed, large deposits accumulated in the Bank of England, money dealers having vast sums lent to them upon call were themselves obliged to resort to the Bank of England for increased supplies, and for some days nearly the whole requirements of commerce were thrown on the bank, when on the 12th of November the Government authorized the bank to disregard the restriction of the bank act. The effect was the same as in 1847. On the 12th, the bank discounted and advanced to the amount of £2,373,000, which still left a reserve of £581,000. The demand for discounts and advances continued to increase till the 21st, when they reached the maximum of £21,616,000. The panic rapidly subsided, and notwithstanding commercial failures of immense magnitude, the crisis passed over without the prostration of our commercial existence. The bullion reached its lowest point on the 18th of November, £6,484,000. The issues beyond the legal limit were only £928,000. On the 1st December, the overissue had been returned to the issue department, having averaged, during the eighteen days, only £488,830."

The failures exceeded £41,000,000, whose deficits were estimated at £7,754,900. That the crisis was not due to overissues of bank notes is self-evident by the fact that the entire circulation of the United Kingdom in 1857 was, in round numbers, only £38,000,000, whereas in 1815 it amounted to £58,771,000. The Liverpool Borough Bank was not a bank of issue, and the entire issues of the Western Bank of Scotland and the City of Glasgow Bank, were only £800,000, against deposits of £9,000,000. In the debates that occurred in Parliament, Mr. Spooner attributed all the monetary derangements and commercial embarrassments to the act of 1844, which he declared to be a delusion. "It had answered none of the expectations held out by its promoters—it could not be amended and must be abolished." Mr. Glyn differed from Mr. S. as to the effect of the act of 1844 upon the commercial crisis, . . . but although the pressure was not caused by the act, the limitation of issues by the bank became, in his opinion, in the time of pressure, the primary cause of the crisis.*

The position of the bank was :

| | Circulation. | Bullion. | Private Securities. | Rate of Discount. |
|---|---|---|---|---|
| 27th June, | £19,819,721 | £11,378,872 | £18,987,886 | 6 |
| 11th July, | 20,702,903 | 11,592,160 | 16,455,171 | 5½ |
| 29th Aug., | 20,108,234 | 11,500,587 | 17,811,663 | 5½ |
| 3d Oct., | 20,824,714 | 10,662,692 | 21,835,843 | 6 |
| 10th " | 20,862,690 | 10,109,943 | 22,398,877 | 7 |
| 17th " | 21,052,315 | 9,524,478 | 20,539,565 | 8 |
| 4th Nov., | 21,071,942 | 8,497,780 | 22,628,251 | 9 |
| 11th " | 21,036,430 | 7,170,508 | 26,113,453 | 10 |
| 18th " | 22,235,954 | 6,484,096 | 30,299,270 | 10 |
| 25th " | 22,156,143 | 7,263,672 | 31,350,717 | 10 |
| 9th Dec., | 20,953,992 | 8,069,489 | 30,111,185 | 10 |
| 23d " | 20,133,558 | 10,753,281 | 28,088,186 | 8 |

We find here that as the bullion decreased, the cir-

* Annual Register, 1857.

culation and loans of the bank increased, and *vice versâ*, the very reverse of the theory on which the act of 1844 is based (and of the result it was intended to produce), which is that circulation and loans will diminish as bullion diminishes, and increase as bullion increases.

The London Economist of 28th November, 1857, says: "From 1819 down to the present time there is no element in the banking statistics of this country which presents such uniformity as that of the bank circulation. The most fluctuating elements in our banking accounts are the amount of bullion held in reserve by the bank, and the amount of capital (credit ?) advanced upon private securities to traders. While circulation is most stationary, the quantity of capital (credit ?) unemployed and employed is most fluctuating. In 1825 the crisis broke out among the London bankers who issued no notes—in Liverpool it was most severely felt where notes had never been issued by any of the banks."

"But if we turn from these scenes of disaster in England to kindred events on the Continent, what do we find ? Why, that on the spot most affected—where the losses are greatest—where the panic is most severe—where, as far as facts have yet been divulged, there exists the strongest presumption that speculation of a reckless kind has been carried to the greatest extent,—there is no paper circulation at all, but that it is one of the only places in Europe which boasts a purely metallic currency :—we mean the Republic of Hamburg. There the rate of interest has fluctuated more, and upon the whole, been higher than in any other part of Europe ; and to such an extent has discredit spread, that the public at large has been obliged to unite and form a guarantee fund, in order to save the commercial community from common ruin arising from panic and distrust." * One hundred and sixty houses suspended payments in Hamburg. Interest there was, in October,

| | | | |
|---|---|---|---|
| 7½ per ct., | while it was 6 per ct. in London, | | |
| 9 " | " " 7 " " | 6½ per ct. in Paris. | |
| 8½ " | " " 8 " " | 7½ " " † | |

As the crisis in England was in a great measure due to the crisis which originated in New York, it becomes interesting to examine the condition of the New York banks. We find the following in the London Economist of the 26th of December, 1857:

"Condition of the banks of the State of New York in

| | June, 1852. | June, 1856. | Sept., 1857. |
|---|---|---|---|
| Capital, | $59,705,000 | $92,334,000 | $107,507,000 |
| Circulation, | 27,940,000 | 30,705,000 | 27,122,000 |
| Deposits, | 65,634,000 | 96,267,000 | 84,529,000 |
| Loans and Discounts, | 127,245,000 | 174,141,000 | 170,846,000 |
| Specie, | 13,304,000 | 18,510,000 | 14,321,000 |

"If ever there were accounts which exhibited moderate and prudent banking we find them in these returns," says the London Economist. What a comment on the hasty and injudicious action of the New York banks, which, when in a condition declared by the highest

* London Economist, 28th November, 1857.

† "It is a favorite doctrine with some persons that it is impossible to have an undue extension of credit with a purely metallic basis, and that an improper issue of bank notes is the sole cause of too great an expansion of credit, just as if the currency being made of metal could prevent people from giving their 'promises to pay,' and buying up goods on speculation." (Macleod, Theory and Practice of Banking, vol. ii, p. 58.)

authority in England, moderate and prudent, at the very moment that the boundless crops of our fertile soil were coming forward to arrest the drain of specie, produced a panic by an unnecessary curtailment of loans, that carried disaster and destruction to the commerce of two continents!

## CHAPTER XI.

Sir Robert Peel's act of 1844 was entirely based on the idea that all speculations, and the commercial reactions that follow them, are caused by expansions of the currency—in other words, on the almost universally admitted theory that the volume of the currency is the measure of values—that an increase in the volume of the currency produces a rise of prices, and a decrease a fall of prices. *This theory is correct if the term currency be made to include bank deposits and the checks drawn against them, bills of exchange, notes of hand, credits of every description; in one word, everything that causes property to pass from hand to hand; everything that increases the demand for it. But it is entirely erroneous if the term currency be intended, as is almost invariably the case, to include only coin and bank notes.** In that sense the theory is not only erroneous

* "The act of 1844 treats currency simply as bank notes to bearer; but they who observe critically and carefully all the varied mazes of our moneyed transactions, must recognize an almost endless variety of objects acting more or less directly and with more or less celerity the same part-bills of exchange at long or short dates—exchequer bills—India and rail-road bonds—deposits on demand with the great money brokers—latterly, post-office orders for small sums passing from town to town, of which useful description of *quasi* currency the public will probably be surprised to learn that little short of £6,000,000 were circulated last year—but above all,

now, but was so even before bank notes and commercial credits were used, for then barter was an important element in the exchanges of commodities, and permitted

deposits, both with the Bank of England and private bankers, are a most essential part of this currency; . . . they are in fact the most formidable means of commanding the treasures of the bank, though they seem to be wholly overlooked by our exclusive guardians of the currency. . . . The theorist sees in circulation nothing but the bank notes; but the practical man, engaged in large operations, knows how many millions pass through his hands without his seeing or touching a bank note, and how many varied securities and engagements perform the essential duties of his circulation." (The Financial or Commercial Crisis Considered, by Lord Ashburton.)

"Whatever confers the power of demanding services or commodities, or professes to confer the power of demanding them, is the currency or circulating medium of any single person, and includes not only the current coin of the realm, but all its substitutes of every description, and whatever else represents or displaces it. Adopting this definition, we may enumerate the different species of it as follows:

"1. Coined money, gold silver and copper.

"2. Bills of exchange, including checks.

"3. Promissory notes, including bank notes.

"4. The sum standing at his credit in his banker's books.

"5. Private debts due him." (Macleod, Theory and Practice of Banking, vol. i, p. 37.)

"But as the relations of commerce extend themselves, and nations advance in industry and wealth, credit becomes gradually a more and more important engine in the mechanism of the social system, and men begin ere long to discover that, by the simple intervention of credit alone, nine tenths of their transactions of purchase and sale may be conveniently and economically adjusted, without any interchange whatever of actual value, whether intrinsic or factitious. Hence the introduction into use of the bank note. But the bank note is only one, and scarcely even the most important, of the various forms in which credit may be employed to facilitate exchanges. And you cannot, therefore, include the bank note under the generic designation of money, without finding yourself immediately embarrassed by the claims of bills of exchange, bankers' checks, and a variety of other typifications of the same principle of credit, all of which being more or less competent to perform, and, in point of fact, performing the functions of money, and some of them on a scale of vast extent, have, *prima facie*, just the

the demand to be greater than the existing amount of money could exchange. If the mere increase of the currency could affect prices, values would not depend on natural laws, but on man's action.

same pretensions to be rated as money which bank notes have." (Fullarton on the Regulation of Currencies, p. 29.)

"There is scarcely any shape into which credit can be cast, in which it will not at times be called to perform the functions of money; and whether that shape be a bank note, or a bill of exchange, or a banker's check, the process is in every essential particular the same, and the result is the same." (Id., ib., p. 37.)

"The purchasing power of an individual at any moment is not measured by the money actually in his pocket, whether we mean by money the metals, or include bank notes. It consists, first, of the money in his possession; secondly, of the money at his banker's, and all other money due to him and payable on demand; thirdly, of whatever credit he happens to possess. To the full measure of this threefold amount, he has the power of purchase. How much he will employ of this power, depends upon his necessities, or upon his expectations of profit. Whatever portion of it he does employ, constitutes his demand for commodities, and determines the extent to which he will act on prices." (J. S. Mill, Westminster Review, June, 1844.)

"We shall not hesitate to adopt some such classification of the constituent parts of the whole volume of negotiable instruments at present in use in this country as the following:

"1, coin; 2, bank notes; 3, checks; 4, bills of exchange; 5, ledger accounts. And to admit the substantial correctness of a doctrine which teaches in effect that coin is the small change of bank notes; bank notes the small change of checks; checks the small change of bills of exchange; and bills of exchange the small change of transactions of sale and purchase, the record of which is contained in a ledger, and the adjustment of which is accomplished mainly by the process of set-off." (Tooke, History of Prices, vol. vi, pp. 593, 594.)

"If it be an undeniable fact, that nine tenths, or some other very large proportion of all the transactions of purchase and sale which take place in the kingdom are adjusted without the intervention of money properly so called at all, and by the use of other expedients of credit than bank notes; and if, lastly, the supply of some of those expedients of credit is increasing and inexhaustible, utterly beyond the reach of legal restraint, and never

But although every representative of money and commodities is capable of performing, and does perform at times, the functions of money, it is not always a portion of the currency. Fullarton says very well: "Every instrument of exchange produces no effect on prices as long as not used to effect purchases. All in-

denied to any one who has occasion to use them and value to give for them, stronger evidence surely cannot well be desired or imagined of the utter hopelessness of any attempt to control those purchases and sales, or the fluctuations of value which they engender, or by any officious tampering with the free supply of so comparatively insignificant a portion of the whole mass of circulating credit as the bank notes, and that portion the least of any in affinity with the great operations of trade by which the course of prices and exchanges is really directed." (Fullarton on the Regulation of Currencies, p. 51.)

"'The circulation of every country may be considered as divided into two different branches—the circulation of the dealers with one another, and the circulation between the dealers and consumers. . . . The value of the goods circulated between the different dealers with one another can never exceed the value of those circulated between the dealers and the consumers, whatever is bought by the dealers being ultimately destined to be sold to the consumers.' (Smith's Wealth of Nations, pp. 141, 142.) "Coin, and the smaller denomination of notes serving as coin, are essential to the exchanges between dealers and consumers, and if these smaller notes are withdrawn, their place must be supplied by coin; but not so as regards the interchange between dealers and dealers. Bank notes are not only not essential to that interchange, but in point of fact, bank notes are rarely used in the larger dealings of sales and purchases. All the transactions between dealers and dealers, by which are to be understood all sales from the producer or importer, through all the stages of intermediate processes of manufacture or otherwise, to the retail dealer or the exporting merchant, are resolvable into movements or *transfers of capital.* Now, transfers of capital do not necessarily suppose, nor do actually, as a matter of fact, entail, in the great majority of transactions, a passing of money, that is, bank notes or coin—I mean bodily, and not by fiction—at the time of the transfer. All the movements of capital may be, and the great majority are, affected by the operations of banking and credit, without the intervention of actual payment in coin or bank notes." (Tooke, History of Prices, vol. iii, pp. 228–230.)

struments drawing interest have a tendency to accumulate in the hands of capitalists as investments, and in that case they no longer act as money. The true light, therefore, in which we ought to regard these various forms of circulating credit is rather as a vast and inexhaustible *fund* of potential currency, at the free command of every man whose exigencies require its aid, and who has an equivalent to render, or security to pledge, in return." * It is from that inexhaustible fund that the community draw the means to effect purchases, whenever they so feel inclined, without the aid of either coin or bank notes; purchases that, by their magnitude, affect prices infinitely more than the moderate ones effected with coin or bank notes.

The following remarks, and official returns of the Bank of England, extracted from the London Economist, are as interesting as they are conclusive:

"It is said that it was excessive issues which produced and mainly caused the convulsions of 1825 and 1837, and therefore they ought to be restricted. Here is obviously a confusion between currency and capital (credit ?)—between the issues of notes and the loan of capital (credit ?)—between circulation and credit. Is it a fact that there were excessive issues at those times? The years 1821, 1822, 1823, and the first half of 1824, were certainly not periods of speculation. Toward the close of 1824 some excitement prevailed, and it increased until the summer of 1825, when it was at its height. A reaction began about September, and it increased into a panic or convulsion in the middle of December, *first, by the suspension of London banks,*

* On the Regulation of Currencies, p. 44.

*who by law were prohibited from issuing notes.* Well, how stood the circulation of the bank during that period? We find the circulation and private securities of the bank to have been:

| | | Circulation. | Private Securities. |
|---|---|---|---|
| 1821 | August | £20,295,000 | £2,722,000 |
| 1822 | February | 18,665,000 | 3,494,000 |
| | August | 17,464,000 | 3,622,000 |
| 1823 | February | 18,392,000 | 4,660,000 |
| | August | 19,231,000 | 5,624,000 |
| 1824 | February | 19,736,000 | 4,530,000 |
| | August | 20,132,000 | 6,255,000 |
| 1825 | February | 20,753,000 | 5,503,000 |
| | August | 19,398,000 | 7,691,000 |

"Is it possible to recognize any proof of excessive issues in these figures? But what is most striking, is, that notwithstanding the slight variations in the circulation during the great excitement of 1825, when speculation was so rash, and credit so indiscriminate, after the greatest possible restriction had been placed upon credit in December and January, the circulation of the bank had risen on the 28th February to £25,467,000.

"Again, let us examine the facts as they existed in 1837, and prior to the convulsion of that year. The years 1833 and 1834, and the first half of 1835, were periods of no excitement or speculation. Toward the close of 1835, the great American speculation set in, and continued during the greater part of 1836. In October of that year, some difficulties began to be experienced, which increased in intensity till the middle of 1837. Well, how stood the circulation during those years? We find it as follows:

| | | Circulation. | Private Securities. |
|---|---|---|---|
| 1833.... | February.... | £19,370,000 | £5,450,000 |
| | August....... | 19,629,000 | 5,999,000 |
| 1834.... | February.... | 19,252,000 | 8,524,000 |
| | August....... | 18,839,000 | 9,683,000 |
| 1835.... | February.... | 18,328,000 | 7,870,000 |
| | August....... | 17,892,000 | 11,068,000 |
| 1836.... | February.... | 18,102,000 | 11,225,000 |
| | August....... | 18,158,000 | 13,197,000 |
| 1837.... | February.... | 18,232,000 | 15,056,000 |

"What proof is there here again of excessive issues having led to the convulsion of 1837? On the contrary, it is curious that at the moment when the great speculation began, in the autumn of 1835, the bank issues were at a lower point than at any time during the whole period. If we refer to the bank returns, we shall easily discover how, upon this explanation, the convulsions of 1825 and of 1837 arose. We shall find that, although the circulation continued almost stationary, the advances by way of loans and discounts rapidly increased, and led to the excitement and indiscriminate credit which in those years led to such disasters.

"The 'private' securities, consisting chiefly of bills discounted, were in August, 1821, only £2,722,000; in August, 1824, they had increased to £6,255,000; and in August, 1825, they had further increased to £7,691,000, showing an entire increase of nearly £5,000,000; and this took place without any increase in the circulation whatever; and yet all the mischief is said to have risen from excessive issues, without any reference to the true cause of excessive loans of capital (credit?)."

"The circumstances which led to the speculations of 1845 and 1847, were very similar to those of the former periods, both in relation to circulation and to advances of capital (credit ?) upon securities. These two elements in the bank returns stood thus:

| | | Circulation. | Private Securities. |
|---|---|---|---|
| 1844.... | February.... | £21,148,000 | £5,837,000 |
| | August....... | 21,485,000 | 7,870,000 |
| 1845.... | February.... | 21,201,000 | 11,809,000 |
| | August....... | 22,109,000 | 11,712,000 |
| 1846.... | February.... | 20,968,000 | 12,242,000 |
| | August....... | 21,390,000 | 12,755,000 |
| 1847.... | February.... | 20,151,000 | 15,819,000 |
| | August....... | 18,828,000 | 16,923,000 |

"It is impossible to examine these facts, without arriving at the conclusion that excessive issues had nothing to do with the panic of 1847, but that, as in 1825 and 1837, excessive credits were the sole cause. So far from the circulation being excessive at the moment the panic arrived in September, 1847, it was lower than it had been at any time during the whole period, but the advances upon private securities had increased from £5,837,000 in 1844, to £16,923,000 in August, 1847."

"Acting upon the fallacious assumption, then, that all over trading and consequent panics have been caused by excessive issues, and that the bank had it in its power to increase or diminish its issues at pleasure, Parliament was induced to pass the act of 1844, the supposed effect of which would be to regulate the currency according to prescribed rules. But experience has shown that, while the bank has every power over the amount of its advances, it has little or none over its circulation. Sir Robert Peel appeared to think that the only means by which bankers could issue notes was by the way of loans or discounts, and that they had therefore the power, by contracting their loans, to contract also the circulation, and by extending their loans permanently to increase the circulation. The slightest consideration will show that both these views were equally unfounded. The bank may at pleasure contract its loans and discounts either by raising the rate of interest, or by refusing accommodation; but the bank cannot contract the circulation at will, so long as it holds large deposits on behalf of the public, which they can withdraw at pleasure. If notes are required for the purposes of circulation, they will be withdrawn by depositors in spite of any attempt of the bank to contract their amount. Indeed, it generally happens when the bank is contracting its credits, the circulation for a time becomes larger in place of smaller. So, on the other hand, the bank cannot extend the circulation at will. It may, indeed, increase its loans and discounts; but if the notes are not required for circulation, they will immediately be returned upon the bank for payment. The actual circulation at any time is determined by the requirements of trade in order to conduct internal exchanges, and not by the will of the issuers of notes. As long as bankers hold large amounts in deposits belonging to the public, the circulation cannot be reduced below the necessary amount required by the convenience of trade, however much bankers may contract their credits, and as long as the notes are payable on demand, the issues cannot be excessive, however imprudent bankers may be in extending their credits."

"Bank notes had, therefore, nothing to do with these convulsions. It must be plain to every intelligent mind that they might equally have happened had there been no bank notes in existence, and if the currency had been purely and exclusively metallic. They were caused by the simple and clear fact that the bank had been led into loans to an imprudent extent."

The statistics in the preceding extracts prove that the circulation of the Bank of England declines in moments of speculation and expansion of credits, while it increases in moments of panic and contraction of credits. The reason of this is, evidently, that when every one has confidence in the future, individual promises to pay circulate with such facility that they replace to a certain extent bank notes, while in moments of distrust each one seeks to possess and to retain bank notes, which are considered perfectly reliable resources at all times and under all circumstances.

## CHAPTER XII.

THE more closely currency is analyzed, the more clearly does it appear that currency is a strictly self-regulating machine, which, if left entirely free, will exactly adapt its volume to the wants of the community. The currency can never be inflated beyond the requirements of the community by paper, as long as it can be repaid to the issuers, and thus arrest the interest paid for their loan.* The volume of the currency is always

* "On the first establishment of a bank of issue, in a district which had not been previously provided with banking accommodation, the command of capital which the banker acquires from the substitution of his notes for the money previously in circulation, and which enables him to diffuse credit and prosperity throughout the neighborhood, is very striking. And people easily fall into the delusion that there is no limit to this power, but that the banker can still go on adding to his notes, and giving a fresh impulse to the prosperity he has created, even after the substitution has been completed, and his paper already fills the channels of circulation. Were this so, it is obvious that what is called over issue would be perpetual; for it never ceases to be the interest and desire of the issuer to send out as many notes as the community will receive from him. It is quite idle to talk, as some reasoners are in the habit of doing, of bankers exercising the privilege of issue at one time with exemplary moderation, and at another with reckless imprudence. There is no such thing. Bankers will be more or less prudent in the *facilities of credit* which they afford to their customers, accord-

the amount held by the entire community in their pockets or in their cash tills ; it never can exceed this. If a country holds more coin than is needed by the community, the surplus will lie idle in the vaults of banks or individual bankers. It is precisely the same with paper currency. If banks issue notes beyond the amount required by the community, the excess returns immediately to the bank of issue for redemption. When banks accumulate large surplus of coin, it is no evidence that the amount of coin in the country has increased. The accumulation may be, and most frequently is, the effect of diminished ability or inclination to exchange commodities, and of its natural consequence, restricted commerce.

Banks should never be made to loan their capital to

ing to the state of their own circumstances, and those of the times; and their advances must necessarily at all times be limited by the means of the bankers. But, whether the bankers' advances be large or small, whether the aspect of the times be cheerful or disheartening, it must be equally his policy to keep out as large a *circulation* as he can. What advances he does make, he will always be anxious to make in his own notes, because they yield him a profit such as no other form of issue yields.

"It may be stated, therefore, as a settled principle, that the efforts of banks of issue to extend their circulation know no remission; that the whole system, in fact, is continually on the stretch; and that, but for the antagonistic force which is always in action to correct and repress it, the overflow of notes would be irresistible. Upon this ground alone, then, there seems to me to be an effectual negative to the supposition that the fluctuations of the bank-note circulation depend on the discretion of the bankers. A man who has already put forth his whole strength, has no further effort left to make. The state of a banker, who has already issued every note which those who deal with him will take from his hands, becomes thenceforth entirely passive. He cannot issue another till there is a fresh demand. And if there be each time a fresh demand, I apprehend there can be no over issue—no redundance which can possibly affect prices." (Fullarton on the Regulation of Currencies, pp. 82, 83.)

the state, nor invest it in state stocks, but should invariably retain it in their own hands. All laws exacting the deposit of state stocks, as security for the redemption of bank notes, are an error, based on the supposition that state stocks are more permanent in their value than other property. History fully proves the error of this theory. Nothing is so permanent in its value, so easily realized in moments of emergency, as good commercial paper, bearing two or more signatures, representing actual transfers of commodities.

Banks of issue loan their promises to pay, or bank notes, drawing no interest, in exchange for individual promises to pay, drawing interest. This interest is the profit of the banks, and their reward for exchanging well-known paper for that but little known, as well as for the risk attending such operations. These exchanges of credits on these conditions, are as advantageous to the individuals as to the banks, for to the individuals, the loan of bank notes is as useful as the loan of a similar amount in coin or capital in any form. Banks of issue, as long as they enjoy undoubted credit, are only forced to contract their loans when the necessities of the community force its members to diminish the amount of bank notes usually carried by them in their pockets or held in their cash drawers. This only occurs at long intervals, after bad harvests or great over trading, and even then not to a great extent. But confidence in the banks once shaken, the notes are rapidly returned, and failures frequently ensue, even of institutions with ample means, which cannot be realized rapidly enough to meet, on presentation, all the liabilities of the banks. As long as the currency is in good credit, there can be no danger to banks of issue in loaning their bank notes *for short periods, and on undoubted securities.* Short loans never lead to over trading, because the borrowers can only use them in operations which will or can be promptly closed. All the difficulties with banks of issue, as well as with banks of deposit, arise from long loans, or from loans on securities which cannot be realized at maturity.

Banks of deposit principally loan credits on their ledgers, bearing no interest, transferable by checks, in exchange for individual promises to pay, bearing interest. Every discount of commercial notes by a bank of deposit becomes at once transformed into deposits, although, in reality, the notes payable at a future day, discounted by the bank, are the only deposit made. And yet it is generally supposed that banks of deposit lend their deposits! Banking on deposits is, like banking on circulation, nothing but the substitution of a well-known credit for one less known. Were banking the loaning of actual capital, as is generally supposed, it would be infinitely less useful than it is. It would merely displace capital—give to one what is taken from another—and this could be done by the individual owner of the capital, without the necessity of the expensive intervention of banking institutions. One of the great advantages offered by banks is, that to the merchants, and others keeping accounts with them, they are precisely what the London clearing house is to the London bankers, and the New York clearing house to the New York banks—a medium of offsetting one claim against another, *without the trouble and expense of resorting to coin or bank notes for every payment.*

The banks, being the reservoirs where the community keep all their floating means, must, at all times, not only possess coin sufficient to liquidate the balances between themselves, but also to liquidate balances with distant points, whenever they occur, until such time as paper money shall circulate, like gold and silver, throughout the entire world. Commerce is simply the exchange of commodities. The ebbs and flows of these exchanges are almost as regular as those of the tides, and, when once properly understood, they can almost always be foreseen and provided for. The realization of the crops of a country is the principal cause of the ebbs and flows of the currency. When the crops are brought to market, the currency must be enlarged; after they are realized, the currency gradually contracts again until the appearance of the next crops. In a country where coin alone circulates, the enlargement of the currency can only proceed from private hoards, gathered when the currency contracts, or when the precious metals are imported from other countries. Where bank notes circulate the enlargement is made by the issue of new notes, which return to the issuers the moment they are no longer needed by the community.

Bad harvests are one of the most powerful causes of disturbance to banking, as well as commercial and industrial operations.* If it be the cereal crops that partially fail, the deficit must be supplied from other countries, mostly in exchange for specie, because the countries from which the cereals are then to be drawn

* "Except in the single instance of 1825, there has not occurred within the last half century a drain of gold of any importance, at all commercial in its origin, to which the importations of corn have not more or less contributed." (Fullarton on the Regulation of Currencies, p. 152.)

cannot at once increase their consumption of the commodities produced by the country needing the cereals; for the consumption of a community is the result of habits, acquired during long periods of time, which are not changed at a moment's notice; and even if the producers of cereals were desirous of increasing at once their consumption of those commodities, the country needing the cereals could rarely furnish them in sufficient quantities to balance, at once, unusually large imports of cereals, for it takes time and preparation to increase largely the supply of any article. If, on the other hand, the deficient harvest be of products usually exported abroad in payment of foreign commodities, coin must supply the deficit in the exportation of products until the importations of foreign commodities are checked.* In either case, commerce and industry—in fact, the whole community—will suffer from the deficient harvest, and bankers should be extremely cautious and prudent in their operations in such moments.†

* "As nothing can be made by moving gold and silver, an influx of gold implies a great abundance and low prices of all other commodities; so an export of gold implies a great scarcity and high price of all other commodities. An export of gold takes place when we have such a diminution in the stock of commodities generally, that it becomes unprofitable to export them to a sufficient extent to pay for our imports."

† "If there has been a failure of the crops, and, to relieve the necessities of the population, three millions of quarters of wheat are to be imported from abroad, so much of the capital of the nation will have to be sacrificed for that object. Whether that capital is transmitted in merchandise or in specie, is a point which in no way affects the nature of the transaction; the corn can only be obtained in exchange for an equivalent, and that equivalent must, in one shape or other, come out of the wealth of the country. The loss is irretrievable; it is the penalty inseparable from a great physical calamity, which must be submitted to; and if any portion of the penalty shall have been paid in gold, that gold can only be got back again

Still, even then, they should not hesitate to loan on ample and undoubted security, for it becomes important, in such moments, that commerce and industry should obtain facilities till they can realize, without undue sacrifice, the commodities they hold on hand: this requires time, and, meanwhile, persons possessed of ample property should not be driven into bankruptcy, because, temporarily, property is difficult to realize. Anything really useful to humanity cannot long remain without demand, and forced sales, at great sacrifices, disorganize industry and commerce, to the great injury of the entire community, and every effort should be made to avert such results.

The evident duty of a bank is, during the period when the currency contracts, to supply the natural demand for loans and circulation, but not to seek to increase it by offering to loan at reduced rates of interest, or to parties offering doubtful securities. And, on the other hand, not to decrease their loans and circulation rapidly when they lose specie. Banks, instead of attempting to keep uniform reserves of specie, should rather see that their reserves are always in proportion to the approaching wants of the community—wants which they should freely supply as long as it is in their power. To merchants, credits on bank ledgers are as useful for their local operations as the same amount in coin, while to the banks the calling in of loans very slightly, if at all, augments their specie reserves. Banks need specie reserves, beyond the small amount used to

by a second exportation of capital, to be created by fresh exertions of industry and given in exchange for it." (Fullarton on the Regulation of Currencies, p. 124).

liquidate the daily balances between each other, only to liquidate an adverse balance of trade with some distant point; and they can only increase their aggregate specie reserves from receipts from those points where the exchanges are in their favor. When banks lose specie, they should remember that this is the result of mercantile operations commenced long before, which no action on their part can then arrest or cancel; that receipts from other points are the only means by which the coin they are losing can be replaced. Many persons suppose that when coin is exported it is invariably to effect with it purchases abroad, whereas it is almost invariably exported to meet purchases made long before.* Contraction of loans and circulation at home is, then, worse than useless; for, instead of strengthening

* Mr. Nicholas Biddle, President of the United States Bank, in an essay published in April, 1828, in the *National Gazette*, of Philadelphia, said: "The law of a mixed currency of coin and paper is, that when, from superabundance of the mixed mass, too much of the coin part leaves the country, the remainder must be preserved by diminishing the paper part, so as to make the mixed mass more valuable in proportion. It is this capacity of diminishing the paper which protects it. . . . The operation proceeds thus: by issuing no new notes, but requiring something from your debtors, *you oblige them to return you the bank notes* you lent them, or their equivalent. This makes the bank notes scarcer—this makes them more valuable —*this makes the goods for which they are generally exchanged less valuable—the debtor, in his anxiety to get your notes, being willing to sell his goods at a sacrifice*—this brings down the price of goods, and makes everything cheaper. Then the remedy begins. The foreigner, finding that his goods must be sold so low, sends no more. The American importer, finding that he cannot make money by importing them, imports no more. . . . When the foreigner hears of this state of things, he sends back the coin he took away. He took it away merely because your own domestic productions were so high that he could not make any profit in his country by taking them. But when the news reaches him that his productions are very cheap in our country, he will also learn that our productions are cheap

themselves, the banks only reduce the value of all commodities selling to other points, thereby increasing the adverse balance to be liquidated in coin; besides which, sudden contractions produce panics, which universally weaken both banks and their debtors.* An intelligent

too, and he sends back the coin to buy these cheap productions of ours. . . . Such is the circle which a mixed currency is always describing."

"The course of business has been this: A merchant borrows from the banks and sends abroad $100,000 in coin, or he buys bills from one who has shipped the coin. With these he imports a cargo of goods—sends them to auction, where they are sold, and the auctioneer's notes given for them. These notes are discounted by the banks, and the merchant is then put in possession of another $100,000, which he again ships, and thus he proceeds in an endless chain. The constant tendency of banks is to lend too much and to put too many notes into circulation." (Gouge on Banking, pp. 52, 53.)

Here is a man long looked upon as the most eminent financier in the United States, who long presided over one of the largest banking institutions of the world, who proves himself not only ignorant of the principles governing banking, but also of a knowledge of the *modus operandi* of the ordinary operations of commerce; and who deliberately recommends to bankers a course of action which, he says himself, *will reduce the value of the assets of their debtors and force them to make sacrifices!* After this, is it surprising that commercial disasters have been frequent in the United States, and that the institution over which Mr. Biddle presided became itself a bankrupt, leaving not a fraction of the wreck to be saved for the unfortunate owners? How can paper money be beneficial when controlled by men who are entirely ignorant of the principles that govern it?

* "A contraction of the circulation leads to a general apprehension of danger. Hence the bankers and others keep larger reserves of bank notes on hand, in order to be prepared for the worst, and thus the evils of the contraction are considerably increased. That portion of the notes of the Bank of England which is passing from hand to hand, may be called the active circulation. That portion which is hoarded, or kept in reserve to meet possible demands, may be called the dead circulation. Now it is quite certain that the dead circulation, while it remains in that state, has no effect upon the price of commodities, the spirit of speculation, or the foreign exchanges. These are affected only by the active circulation. In seasons of pressure, the dead circulation is increased at the expense of the

banker should neither become elated at one moment nor alarmed at another; if he is conversant, as he should be, with the natural laws that control commerce, currency, and banking, he will know that they regulate themselves. Any attempt, on his part, to interfere with the operations of commerce, only aggravates existing evils. Importations and exportations are made by individuals, solely with a view to the profit to be derived from them. Whenever either are in excess of the necessities or the means of consumption of the communities for which they are destined, the expected profits are turned into losses, and this soon arrests new operations, until the equilibrium between supply and demand be reëstablished, without any intervention on the part of bankers or Government. Supply and demand are the natural regulators of commerce and industry, and, like every natural law, they act far more beneficially for man than any laws of his own making. Unfortunately, few persons have faith in these laws, because they have no knowledge of them, and ignore the admirable results they produce; they therefore resort to human reglementations, which invariably end by being injurious instead of beneficial. The only possible measure in accordance with the law of supply and demand that can be resorted to by banks, is to increase or diminish the rate of interest on loans in proportion to the demand; but from this proper action the Ameri-

active circulation, because people hoard their money to meet contingencies. Hence we find the pressure is often more severe than the reduction of the bank circulation would seem to warrant. But the fact is that the pressure is in proportion to the reduction of the *active circulation*, and not in proportion to the reduction of the whole circulation." (Gilbart, The History of Banking in America, p. 96.)

can banks are debarred by our injurious usury laws. In Europe, at present, it is only by an increase or decrease of the rate of interest on loans that banks attempt to interfere with the supply or demand of money.*

Every general rise of prices is solely produced by confidence, and every general fall of prices by want of confidence, in the future.† When the community, from any cause, have full confidence in the future, the holders of property are not desirous to realize ;‡ every one seeks to purchase, and finds means to do so, to a greater or lesser extent, without any assistance from banks, because most commercial purchases are made on

* "The true method of regulating the paper currency is by regulating the rate of discount. It was by neglecting this that all the great monetary crises were brought on." (Macleod, Theory and Practice of Banking, vol. ii, p. 302 )

† "It is this sudden failure of confidence and extinction of credit, which produces what is called in commercial language a 'pressure on the money market,' and which causes money to be 'tight.' When money is said to be scarce, it does not mean that there is a smaller quantity of money actually in existence than before ; . . . but a great amount of credit which served as a substitute, and was an equivalent for money, is extinguished, and the money is called suddenly to fill the void." (Id., ib., vol. i, p. 229.)

"It is, therefore, not the scarcity of money, but the extinction of confidence, which produces a pressure on the money market; and an examination of all the great commercial crises in this country will show that they have always been preceded and produced by a destruction of this credit, which has usually been brought about by extravagant over trading and wild speculations." (Id., ib., vol. i, p. 231.)

‡ "A falling market will always be well supplied, because people who must sell hasten to do so before the price falls still lower, and buyers hold aloof, waiting as long as they can, to see the lowest. On the other hand, when markets are rising, the case is reversed. The sellers hold aloof, hoping the price will still be higher; and buyers crowd in, hastening to purchase before the price rises more." (Id., ib., vol. i, p. 232.)

credit, and it it is only when the credits become due that the banks are called upon for loans.* A general demand naturally produces a general rise of prices, until something occurs that creates doubt as to the future. Then, at once, nearly every one seeks to realize property; purchasers are found with difficulty, and a general fall of prices ensues. The amount of coin or of bank notes in circulation has little or nothing to do with these ebbs and flows of prices, for at present most of the large commercial transactions are made by means of representatives of money and commodities, such as checks on banks and bankers, bills of exchange, notes of hand, credits on ledgers, &c., &c., and not with coin or bank notes.† Some faint idea of the importance of

* "A demand for increased discounts at the Bank of England is rarely, if ever, felt in the early stages of a speculative tendency, or as a means of making purchases, with a view to a further advance. It is chiefly when a pause takes place in the expected advances, and still more after the commencement of a fall, that the applications for discount become urgent, for the purpose of enabling the parties to meet engagements entered into some time before, and for which they may be supposed to have reckoned on funds to have been realized by advantageous sales." (Tooke, History of Prices, vol. i, p. 196, note.)

† "Excepting indigo and cochineal, the prices of produce, home and foreign, were lower, and in most cases considerably so, in November, 1842, when the circulation had for four of five months averaged £20,000,000, than in the preceding January, when it was, and for some months had been, scarcely over £16,000,000." (Id., ib., vol. iii, p. 49.)

"When the amount of bank notes in circulation had been reduced to the narrowest limits, when the exchanges were low (high), and the bullion in the bank at a minimum, and when credit was most restricted, and the rate of interest unusually high, prices, which, by the currency theory, should have been found down, were, generally, higher than ordinary. And when the former conditions were all, without exception, reversed—when the bank-note circulation had been increased by the addition of more than one third to its previous amount, when the exchanges were high (low) and rising (falling), the bullion in the bank greater in amount than it had been

these means of exchanging commodities may be formed from the following figures:

The annual exchanges at the clearing house of London, which do not comprise the enormous operations of the Bank of England, are estimated at from 1,500 to 2,000 millions sterling:

| | |
|---|---|
| Take the average of these figures, and we have.... | $8,750,000,000 |
| The exchanges at the New York clearing house average, in ordinary times, about $25,000,000 per day (latterly they have averaged nearly double that amount), say per annum.................. | 7,750,000,000 |
| Total amount of annual exchanges at the London and New York clearing houses............... | $16,500,000,000 |

The entire present annual production of the precious metals is estimated at $200,000,000, say about 1⅕ per cent. of the exchanges effected at the clearing houses of London and New York. What then must be the proportion between the annual production of the precious metals and the aggregate exchanges of the whole world? And what must be the proportion between any conceivable reduction or expansion of the bank notes in circulation, and a moderate reduction or expansion of the enormous operations made with paper representatives of commodities and money? When

for many years, and still increasing, when credit was almost unlimited, and the market rate of interest had for two years barely exceeded two per cent. per annum, or less than half its previous amount, prices, instead of being higher, were, with hardly a solitary exception, considerably lower than at the former period."

"No amount of ingenuity of comment could add to the force of the argument against the supposed influence of the amount of the bank-note circulation, or of the rate of interest upon prices, conveyed by a simple statement of these facts." (Tooke, History of Prices, vol. iii, pp. 61, 62.)

we look at these figures we can no longer wonder that the large influx of gold from California and Australia has produced no permanent effect on prices,* and that the expansions and contractions of bank issues have no permanent effect on the prices of labor and commodities.

If the immense operations of commerce and industry are now effected more easily and more economically with paper representatives of money and commodities than with money itself, is it not evident that bank notes can successfully be made to replace coin in all transactions? That the substitution of paper money for coin is exceedingly advantageous to humanity there can be no doubt, provided the paper money be left to the untrammelled management of private interest. The metallic currency of the country is so much capital rendered unproductive in order to increase the productiveness of the remainder. If an instrument less costly can effect the exchanges as well as coin, the capital at present invested in coin will at once become available for productive employment, besides which the wear and tear of the coin will be economized. The coin in the world was estimated by Humboldt in 1827 at £344,000,000 or $1,720,000,000. This amount must have been greatly increased since 1827, but 6 per cent. for wear and tear and interest, on even that amount, is $103,-

* "It is impossible to affirm that the range of general prices has been sensibly raised by the mere operation, in the form of metallic money of even the £160,000,000 or £170,000,000 of new gold introduced into the commercial world. All the instances of an important variation in prices, comparing 1857 with 1851, admit of being accounted for by circumstances affecting the supply or the demand." (Tooke, History of Prices, vol. vi, p. 224.)

200,000 per annum, which would become available for the well being and future progress of humanity, the moment that paper money successfully and entirely replaces the precious metals as a circulating medium. That this desirable result will be attained seems certain. It is a mere question of time, and will depend greatly on the general intelligence of humanity, and still more on the general recognition of the important truth *that the well being and progress of humanity is entirely dependent on individual effort and intelligence, and not on the acts of governments* (protection to life, liberty, and property alone excepted) ; for until that truth be admitted and acted upon by governments, they will continue to attempt to control the issues of paper money, which will prevent humanity from deriving from this admirable instrument, all the benefits it is capable of conferring.

If it were once generally and clearly understood that money is a mere instrument that facilitates the exchanges of commodities and services, and that the great desideratum of a proper circulating medium is, not its redemption in gold and silver, but its redemption by (which means its acceptance in exchange for) commodities and services, the forced redemption of bank notes in coin might be entirely dispensed with, and, along with specie redemption, will inevitably disappear financial panics such as, heretofore, have so frequently occurred, often in the midst of an unusual abundance of commodities, solely from fear of an inadequate supply of money, of an instrument only useful as a means of obtaining the very commodities of which there exists a glut ! Can anything be more absurd than to be panic stricken from fear of the lack of a symbol, when we possess in abundance the very things it symbolizes? Whenever bank notes shall cease to be redeemable in coin on demand, they will be freely issued to those who will pay interest for them and furnish ample security for their return within a specified time. The return of bank notes in repayment of loans is an ample and proper means of redeeming them, and will always prevent the currency from becoming redundant. There will then always be an adequate supply of money—prices will become regular, as they will be solely controlled by cost of production and supply and demand—and we shall no longer see commodities sacrificed and commerce and industry disorganized, merely because the controllers of money refuse to furnish a supply adequate to effect the current exchanges of commodities and services.

Is not this a result to be desired? And can it be attained by any other means than by the general dissemination of a correct knowledge of the natural laws that govern so perfectly and so beneficially, not only money and currency, but all other things that contribute to the well being and progress of humanity; laws that form the subject matter of the science of Political Economy?

THE END.

www.ingramcontent.com/pod-product-compliance
Lightning Source LLC
LaVergne TN
LVHW050528100826
845148LV00002B/480